EXPERIENTIAL MARKETING

EXPERIENTIAL MARKETING

Myths and Realities

Subhashini Kaul

Viva Books
New Delhi | Mumbai | Chennai | Kolkata
Bengaluru | Hyderabad | Kochi | Guwahati

Publisher's note

Every possible effort has been made to ensure that the information contained in this book is accurate at the time of going to press, and the publisher and author cannot accept responsibility for any errors or omissions, however caused. No responsibility for loss or damage occasioned to any person acting, or refraining from action, as a result of the material in this publication can be accepted by the editor, the publisher or the author.

Every effort has been made to trace the owners of copyright material used in this book. The author and the publisher will be grateful for any omission brought to their notice for acknowledgement in the future editions of the book.

First Published 2010

Viva Books Private Limited

4737/23, Ansari Road, Daryaganj, New Delhi 110 002
Tel. 42242200, 23258325, 23283121, Email: vivadelhi@vivagroupindia.net

76, Service Industries, Shirvane, Sector 1, Nerul, Navi Mumbai 400 706
Tel. 27721273, 27721274, Email: vivamumbai@vivagroupindia.net

Jamals Fazal Chambers, 26 Greams Road, Chennai 600 006
Tel. 28294241, 28290304, Email: vivachennai@vivagroupindia.net

B-103, Jindal Towers, 21/1A/3 Darga Road, Kolkata 700 017
Tel. 22816713, Email: vivakolkata@vivagroupindia.net

7, GF, Sovereign Park Aptts., 56-58, K. R. Road, Basavanagudi, Bengaluru 560 004
Tel. 26607409, Email: vivabangalore@vivagroupindia.net

101-102, Moghal Marc Apartments, 3-4-637 to 641, Narayanguda, Hyderabad 500 029
Tel. 27564481, Email: vivahyderabad@vivagroupindia.net

First Floor, Beevi Towers, SRM Road, Kaloor, Kochi 682 018
Tel. 0484-2403055, 2403056, Email: vivakochi@vivagroupindia.net

232, GNB Road, Beside UCO Bank, Silpukhuri, Guwahati 781 003
Tel. 0361-2666386, Email: vivaguwahati@vivagroupindia.net

www.vivagroupindia.com

ISBN: 978-81-309-1475-6

Published by Vinod Vasishtha for Viva Books Private Limited
4737/23 Ansari Road, Daryaganj, New Delhi 110 002

Printed & bound by Raj Press, R-3, Inderpuri, New Delhi 110 012

Contents

Acknowledgements

The need for a book explaining the 'myths and realities' of Experiential Marketing was brought to my notice by many practitioners and students over the last two years. I am grateful to all of them in motivating me to make this effort. I sincerely hope this is reasonably close to their expectations and qualifies as a 'slim volume, simple language book that explains both concepts and concept application'!

I would like to acknowledge contributions specifically by Manasi Shah Marfatia, Academic Associate at IIM Ahmedabad, for her initial draft on issues covering evolution of Experiential Marketing in Chapter 2 and Nirmesh Mehta, PGP II at IIMA for undertaking a non-credit independent project under my guidance that beautifully demonstrated the effectiveness of script-based interviews as mentioned in Chapter 8.

Subhashini Kaul
Head – CARMA
Cheiron People Consulting

1 Introduction

Marketing is once again making a huge change in its course. The last time that happened was several decades ago when product-based segments moved over and gave way to customer-defined market spaces. Half a century ago, a toothpaste marketer was simply in the business of marketing toothpaste. He could not be confused with a toothbrush marketer. He definitely and most certainly was not to be confused with a service marketer. Toothpaste, according to traditional marketers, was a product as distinct from toothbrushes as it was from services such as airline travel which needed a consumer to be around during distribution and delivery. Toothpaste could be stocked and consumed later while a service could not. Services were intangible, unseen. Services needed consumer participation to enable them, while products could be seen and touched and consumer did not have to be actively present during distribution.

When modern marketers stepped in, they revised this divide between products and services – calling it an artificial producer-perspective divide. Modern marketers cursed this unsupported but enduring divide between products and services created by producers and traditional marketers. They lamented that this divide was not based on the perspective of consumer needs and benefits at all. They argued consistently that all products were ultimately bought and used by consumers to deliver some benefits through their service upon usage. In other words, toothpaste was bought by consumers to provide the benefit of clean teeth, fresh breath, healthy gums and so on. The modern marketers were adamant that sensible and useful segmentation could not be based on whether a producer thinks he is offering a product or a service. Instead, market segmentation is to be based on what benefits consumers seek from that offering (be it a product or a service). Benefit-based segmentation came into being as a superior way of looking at the market. Starting with benefit assessments helped marketers figure out what all benefits are sought by different types of consumers. Defining the so-called toothpaste market as that of 'healthy gums' and 'whiter teeth' helped a marketer select who he would target and how he would plan the ground level action while marketing toothpaste.

The smarter modern marketers (who also worried about growth possibilities for a firm) then insisted that the toothpaste market space be defined as that of 'oral hygiene'. This more holistic market definition would help the company's future growth plans, in deciding what new products to offer which would complement the toothpaste offering and help the company stay one step ahead of competition. So a toothpaste marketer was encouraged to extend the existing toothpaste brand equity into toothbrushes, oral rinse, dental floss and so on covering the entire oral hygiene market.

Eventually, all toothpaste marketers did precisely this – benefit segmentation, consumer need assessment, target market selection and sensible expansion with a range of products in the market of 'oral hygiene'. And yet, after several decades, few toothpaste marketers have been able to develop a loyal set of consumers or a community of regular users who are also acting as their brand ambassadors. The entire fight seemed to have only changed the battlefield but not the blunt tools of business warfare.

Experiential Marketing (EM) argues that actually a toothpaste marketer is just that – a toothpaste experience provider. Shocking, is it? Does it seem that this is regressing back to viewing toothpaste as a product? Indeed not! The key is in the focus on 'experience' rather than the offering being a product or a service. The Experiential Marketer is focused on the experience that the offering provides. The experience-centric view puts 'consumer value' back into focus and in much clearer focus than it has ever been before. It goes beyond benefit segmentation and growth through introduction of related products. EM addresses the consumer as a 'whole' individual, not as one part piece consumer of oral hygiene benefits. The growth possibilities for the EM practitioner are not limited in terms of related product category offerings. Growth possibilities are in fact limitless.

EM is closer to the reality of the consumer, and as a body of marketing principles it is thus superior to any other theory till date. EM helps a marketer make true friends with the consumer. EM affords real possibilities to develop and retain a whole community of consumers who are loyal and who connect to the brand in a way that is fulfilling and inherently rewarding to both consumers and the organization. EM regards even the marketer's organization in a 'holistic' manner.

Managing consumer experience is 'destined to become the key and perhaps the only differentiator in the future for business organizations'[1]. Modern marketers (who henceforth we shall pompously call as 'traditional marketers' given the much higher springboard of Experiential Marketing under our feet now!) are beginning to realize this. However, little is understood about the principles of Experiential Marketing though several uninformed and partially informed opinions abound across the globe.

All chapters of this book are written to help unravel the mystery of EM to the EM-uninitiated but otherwise seasoned marketer – whether a practitioners or a students of marketing. The chapters reintroduce the marketer-reader to some long-forgotten and even unexplored principles of marketing. They question current notions of where consumer value is created. They record and raise clear doubts about several well-accepted measures of commonly understood constructs such as consumer value and service quality. They afford insights about consumers that a seasoned marketer always 'knew' as existing but had simply 'forgotten' to look for them, because the world outside propagated a different and more rational way. There is much about EM that we still need to understand. However, this book on EM provides certain strategic alternatives for companies hitherto hidden in the secret annals of academic research and brings all that knowledge out for practitioners and students wanting to understand and apply EM.

This book describes the key principles of Experiential Marketing. It has been written with both marketing practitioners and marketing students in mind. It lists the myths and realities of EM. Myths are exploded using critical thought and logical questioning about practical applications. Realities of EM are stated clearly, so that a reader can appreciate both the scope and the limitations of EM. The simple enunciation of EM principles in this book will help a marketer to plan and execute EM in his or her organization. The numerous examples clarify how EM can be applied effectively to all spheres of marketing – from executing the smallest of marketing tactics to designing the grandest strategic growth plans. For marketing students and academics, the theoretical premises of EM are briefly but well described in this book with copious references. Teachers can use this book and references to design a new elective in EM. Students can use this book as a stepping stone to set their research agenda in the field of EM.

EM is completely anchored with the consumer perspective and abandons all existing premises that lead one away from the consumer. It provides inputs on how a sustainable and constantly growing brand-consumer relationship can be formed based on managing consumer experiences.

References

1. Arussy Lior (2002), *The Experience: How to Wow your Customers and create a Passionate Workplace*, CMP Books, CA, p10-11
2. Shaz Smilansky (2009), *Experiential Marketing – A practical guide to interactive brand experiences*, Kogan Page, London
3. Schmitt Bernd (1999), *Experiential Marketing - How to get Customers to Sense, Feel, Think, Act, Relate*, The Free Press, NY
4. Schmitt Bernd (2003), *Customer Experience Management*, John Wiley and Sons, NJ
5. Lenderman Max (2006), *Experience the Message: How Experiential Marketing Is Changing the Brand World*, Carroll and Graf Edition

2 Myths Surrounding Experiential Marketing

It is almost impossible to find anyone in present times who has not heard of Experiential Marketing and does not have at least a tentative idea of what EM is all about. Yet this field is riddled with myths and unfounded notions. One of the strongest myths surrounding Experiential Marketing (EM) is that it is a recent and phenomenal discovery about consumers, and a startlingly new paradigm in marketing. EM is considered by many discoursing about it to be a newfound orientation of marketers to 'connect' with consumers in increasingly meaningful ways. Several EM proponents, perhaps embarrassed by the ignorance, wilful or otherwise of their proponent brethren, have tried to step away from the hearty jingoism and titled EM as a new 'methodology' rather than a new 'paradigm'. Unfortunately, EM is more than just a new methodology as much as it is not a revolutionary new paradigm. The truth of EM is that marketing researchers and visionary practitioners have been making strident calls for examining the entirety of consumption experience, both in orientation and methods, for several decades now! And EM only calls for marketers to do what marketing has always wanted them to do – connect with the consumers meaningfully.

Unfortunately, these enthusiastic proponents of EM, who have contributed so much to bringing this ignored field of marketing inquiry to the forefront in present times have also considerably regressed inquiry in this field by simply denying the already existing scientific principles and knowledge of EM. Almost all existing popular books on the subject are merely individual authors' discourses and opinions. These books are packaged with rhetoric and newly copyrighted jargon to capture a reader's bemused imagination rather than shape informed practice and further research. Event managers would have you believe that EM is about orchestrating events around the brand, advertisers want you to believe that it is a revolutionary new communication tool, research agencies want you to stand convinced that EM requires a special research plan that only they can prepare for you. Outdoor trainers want you to believe their version of EM and the numerous budding EM consultants frankly want you to remain confused. This confusion is rampant in the US and Europe, little wonder that here in India we have currently about two opinions and twenty versions of each opinion.

This chapter outlines the historical evolution of Marketing in India and establishes the need for Experiential Marketing in specific. The evolution of EM indicates that a call for examining the consumer from the experiential perspective has been around for long but for several reasons the call never picked up before. The call for EM has picked up in present times like wildfire because there is far too much of advertising clutter and far too little of spare time for consumers to pay attention to another 10-second spot on television. Loyalty to almost everything is eroded – whether brands or distribution channels or communication channels. With the rise of internet popularity, social networking sites have risen as influential sources of word-of-mouth promotion that a marketer can neither control nor predict. People have access to multiple sources of information about a brand which a marketer may not even be aware of. Consumers are increasingly demanding of all brands, increasingly impatient with incompetent brands and increasingly slippery even with competent brands. The rise and popularity of EM is hardly surprising in this context.

Any new field of inquiry starts with many ideas and numerous opinions and is naturally marked by much uneasy confusion and doubts. This chapter describes the evolution of EM to anchor the reader to past works and existing scientific knowledge in this field. Then the myths surrounding EM are summarized briefly. The objective is to enable the sincere reader to revisit and abandon any preconceived notions about EM before proceeding to subsequent chapters.

2.1 Evolution of Marketing Focus in India

The concept of branding moved from cattle to businesses when families in Europe found that 'labelling' their products (and hotels such as Hilton) with their family-name helped increase sales. The family-name stood for product quality, and their product quality enhanced the family name in return. Branding was thus a way to help consumers 'recognize' the origin of a product and thus be assured of its quality. The British businessmen replicated this concept of branding in Indian markets as well where in any case small businesses were known by family names & Sons. In the period from 1930s to 1950s, the motivation for branding was to separate oneself from other manufacturers. A branded product stood as an identification mark of quality and performance. Figure 2.1 shows how advertisements only sought to propagate a brand name as a mark of identification, howsoever meaninglessly. Sometimes the brand was hardly visible in the ad (see Valet Safety Razor which is hardly visible at the bottom right corner of the ad), but it was sufficient that the product was branded and the brand's existence was communicated to consumers. Consumers made an active effort to gather information about a newly advertised brand for there were so few around. The latest introductions would get discussed amongst families and friends in the neighbourhood and at the workplace. To not know of the latest brands and the ad line of these brands (if any) was reflective of your ignorance.

Figure 2.1: The advent of branding as an identification mark

Just propagating a brand name: a bicycle ad from 1930s

Ad for Valet Auto-Strop Safety Razor, TOI Annual 1930; Artwork W.S. Bagdatopulos

Brand gave a quality assurance:a soap ad from the 1930s

These initial brand communications just meant to say 'Here I am and that should be enough for you'. And it indeed was enough. Branded products were invariably a little expensive (all that advertising had to be added to the cost-plus pricing scheme right?). Consumers would choose a branded product over unbranded versions simply to reduce risk of poor performance. An advertised brand (with basic quality assurance) thus brought in returns that justified such brand-attention-seeking behaviour. The sole aim of any quality entrepreneur was to become capable of advertising and then all marketing woes were over so long as the distribution and delivery systems kept pace with the increased demand.

Over a period of time, barring pockets of exceptions, most industries emerged with several brands which were comparable in quality related assurances. As industries progressed far beyond being a commodity and became an amalgam of several branded key players, the concept of brand as merely an identification mark had to be abandoned. Branding as a strategy in itself lost meaning. Simply creating a mark of recognition paid no dividends to a company. There was a need to examine alternative routes to attracting consumers to one's brand. The most obvious effort by marketers was now to increase the functional performance of their respective brands. The effort was to get their brand to do more functionally on the key benefit dimension that an offering stood for, thus stand differentiated amongst competing brands and thereby sell more (see Figure 2.2). Thus a tea brand was better if it had stronger liquor and hence was more refreshing (tea was only for refreshment, right?). A shampoo was better if it had more lather and so hair became cleaner (shampoos are only for cleaning the hair, right?). And fans were better if they had more cooling power (what else did a consumer want of a fan?).

Figure 2.2: Branding based on functional superiority implying greater benefits to target consumers

Functional orientation became the focus for a short while but that route too ended abruptly. For one, such enhancements of quality were rather replicable and seldom led to any meaningful competitive advantage. Over a period of time, all competing brands in trying to nudge each other in the race to stay ahead simply moved up the quality ladder together. Secondly, consumers, who were now assured about all competing brands meeting their basic quality expectations, were selecting the brand that best appealed emotionally with them or if none did (as was usually the case), then on price. It was getting impossible to convince consumers that an X brand of toothpaste helped make a significant difference to teeth compared to competing brands that held equally good promise of functional quality.

At around this time marketers caught up with the concept of benefit-based segmentation from the more advanced souls in the US and elsewhere where it was already prevalent. Marketers sought to address each benefit-based segment with an appropriate USP. The end of 1970s ushered in the age of USPs in India. Every brand sought to imbibe itself with a unique proposition that had hitherto not been thought of by competitors. The USP route promised greater benefits as sought by the consumer (see Figure 2.3). The USP route led to a soap being better if it had special oils that made skin softer (targeted at consumers seeking the benefit of soft and glowing skin apart from cleanliness of course); a cold cream was superior if it had almond oil (for consumers who wanted the benefit of beauty apart from the basic purpose of skin protection in winters); and a toothpaste was uniquely wonderful if it had clove oil (which protected gums apart from keeping teeth clean which all toothpastes did).

The USP age stayed for long as it afforded plenty of scope to experiment and discover a new ingredient to attract a particular segment. Soon however, USPs in each brand submerged the hapless consumer. Toothpastes came in various forms – as cream and gel and a mix of both, in red, blue or green and also in a mix of several colours, with whitening crystals or salt or medicinal neem, as minty or clove tasting and also a mix of several flavours. Differences between 'segments' and 'niches' became confused and perhaps irrelevant. The mantra was to have a USP. Fan brands claimed they were better in providing the promised benefit (such as of longer life, trouble-free performance, designer looks, colours, etc. since cooling power was presumed about all fans by now) because they had PSP, which was followed by PSPO and then some more equally vague acronyms. Shampoos picked up this game and soon were imbued with ZPT and then ZPTO. Industry after industry dumped abstract technology abbreviations at the consumer in the name of USP. For a while the Indian consumer tried to keep track of these acronyms and make sense of them. When they stopped making sense, the consumer went back to judging on prices.

Figure 2.3: Branding based on benefit segmentation and USPs

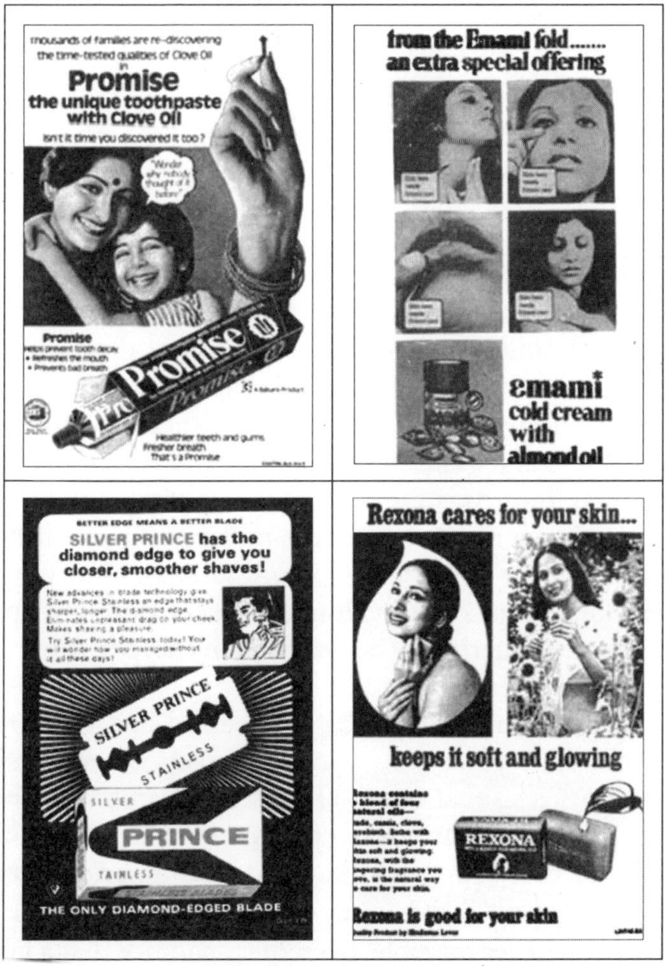

The mid 90s heralded liberal markets in India where brands simply proliferated in the span of just a few months. Rising incomes and, consequently, consumption-related spending increased dramatically. Consumers wanted more variety, the right to choice and certainly the right to quality. Local, regional, national and international brands grew like mushrooms in a fertile forest. By the end of the century it was no longer a sign of ignorance for an educated Indian to be unaware of new brands. The accompanying explosion in technology made information about brands accessible as and when an urban consumer desired it. There was no reason to 'stock-up' on information just in case it was needed later on. Both these reasons added significantly to reduce consumer attention to new brands.

This lack of attention to any brand communicating with them, unless they were predisposed to 'listening', caused traditional media failure with consumers. And in the ensuing confusion about brands, consumers again started doing what they are best at when unsure – they started experimenting with all available brands when possible, otherwise they decided on price which they were still capable of assessing. The advent of modern retailing in India only hastened these inevitable price comparisons. Larger the brand offtake, more was the volume discount and lower was the price at which retailers offered it to consumers. Large retail stores were no longer necessarily more expensive than the inexpensive looking *kiranas*. They were often cheaper. Good brands were no longer necessarily more expensive than unbranded offerings. They were often cheaper. More for less became a consumer expectation.

Brand positioning efforts in this period had no particular sight in mind, no place they wanted to reach. Sales promotions and discounts, seasonal sales, off-season price offs etc., became a norm. Even hitherto-loyal consumers who had sufficient disposable income to not care much about minor price differences changed shopping behaviour. They would postpone their purchases whenever possible given the assurance that a lucrative promotional offer would inevitably come their way within a month. Marketer efforts at using humour, sex and creative art direction in advertising to gain attention abound. These ads were meant to grab consumer attention and tactically convey the brand's continued existence in the clutter, otherwise the efforts were not strategically oriented (see Figure 2.4). The ads were often recollected by consumers but not necessarily the brands themselves. The first signs of a marketer feeling strategically lost in the woods were beginning to show. The effort was simply to garner some of that precious consumer attention by any way for today. Tomorrow was a mere thought, a long foggy way ahead.

Figure 2.4: Increased use of creative appeals in ads primarily to capture elusive consumer altention

Creative appeal for a bicycle

After nearly half a century of concerted branding efforts, firms found themselves back to the marketing dark ages when price was the only consideration in unbranded commodity markets!

2.1.1 Turning to Experiential Marketing

Marketers find the whole concept of 'experience management' as a new hope. The term 'experience' has become so commonly attached to everything nowadays. Mostly it is used as a simply substitute for the USP concept. More informed practice is required. Experiential Marketing is not a mere tool to wield in your media plan and advertising execution. It is not to be adopted as a tactical short-term intervention if long-term benefits are expected. EM needs to be understood as an orientation, a marketing philosophy that stretches from strategic to tactical issues, from not just communication issues (what many proponents fondly call as creating memorable 'live brand experiences') but also in terms of design, production and distribution of the offering.

2.2 Genesis of Experiential Marketing

2.2.1 The Brand Personality

Image centric brand research started in the US somewhere in the late 70s and 80s. Image research was founded on the discovery that brands had taken on a life by themselves. Loyal consumers described their favourite brands as if the brand was imbued with human traits that they themselves possessed or admired. Brand image/personality emerged as the key to building loyalty. A successful brand was one that portrayed humanistic qualities and connected with the consumer. This knowledge transferred to some Indian marketers and has found limited application in the last decade or so in India.

2.2.2 The Consumer Self-Concept

What is little known (or known but not clearly understood) by several marketers is the process by which brand personification works. Brand image research has led to the discovery that brand perceptions are largely influenced by consumer self-image. Consumer self-image (or what we today call as the consumer self-concept) refers to how a consumer perceives herself or himself as a person. The self-image/self-concept is of central importance to an individual consumer. Normal adults plan and direct all day-to-day behaviour to simply maintain and enhance their own self-concept. In this endeavour, people use products and services as symbols reflecting their self-concept. 'Seema, Jaya *aur* Sushma' buy a particular washing powder not because of the brand personality per se, but because of how that brand personality interacts with their own self-concept. This is a discovery about human nature that has far reaching implications for marketers.

Creation of a brand personality is executed in present Indian markets 'just because' and not as a strategic component within a larger vision. Brand personality is a key strategic decision and has to combine with several other strategic aspects. It cannot and will not function in isolation. Marketers need to critically employ this knowledge (about the strong association between brand image and consumer self-concept) to create brand personalities that have meaning for consumers. This cannot be done appropriately unless a marketer is well-informed about the self-concept, its various dimensions and the process of how consumers build relationships with brands. This understanding is the first step to implementing Experiential Marketing.

2.2.3 The Emotional Aspects of Consumption

Till date the informed effort in marketing continues to be towards creating a strong brand personality largely in vacuum. Several firms have tried and failed. Others have succeeded for reasons that they can only explain post hoc (because success needs little explanation anyways!). Even after two decades there are no key principles that can guide a marketer towards creating a successful brand persona. This field of marketing is still largely in the realm of experimentation and intuitive hit-and-trial. One key reason has been that somewhere in the 70s and 80s, when image research was in full swing, the knowledge gained about holistic consumption and emotions of consumers got ignored.

Why did holistic consumption research findings get ignored? It is perhaps best described as the way life is. Truth is often ignored and stays buried until a well-accepted falsehood becomes impossible to sustain anymore. People believed the earth to be the centre of the world for centuries till sufficient data was amassed which made that premise untenable. No one rose any longer to defend the old 'earth-is-the-centre-of-the-universe' premise and so the alternative truth was able to emerge. Such crisis in existing knowledge needs to occur before new premises and alternative explanations find fertile grounds. Scientific enquiry into a new field requires partial abandonment of the existing paradigms. EM is the result of a similar crisis in existing knowledge. Assumptions about a rational consumer are no longer tenable. Consumer behaviour is seldom explainable even for large ticket items using rational decision-making theories. Alternatives are desperately needed by researchers and academics. Consumer research using quantitative survey-based methods are no longer useful. Alternatives are desperately needed by practitioners. Consumer value using benefit-based segmentation is not helping generate loyalty and neither does it provide any clues on how to enhance the offering to generate loyalty. Associating brand personality with the benefit segmentation approach is not helping brands become stronger or live longer. Huge spends on creating brand personalities are going down the drain as targeted consumers seldom even pay attention to brand communications. Academics and practitioners need alternative explanations that take into account the surrounding reality that stares stark in our faces. The reality staring stark in our faces is that traditional marketing principles have simply failed in present times.

2.3 Historical Knowledge of Experiential Marketing

What was ignored by all of us and what has now caught our combined attention is the emotional aspect of consumption. Image research has already given us the understanding that in the brand-consumer interaction process:

- A distinct individualistic pattern of emotional arousal is experienced by the consumer throughout the consumption process.
- The pattern varies for the same consumer across consumption situations and changes with time.
- This emotional arousal is influenced by the perceived brand promise as well as its actual usage. The arousal continues into aspects of post-usage disposal as well. In other words, the emotional arousal is experienced pre-purchase, during and after purchase as well as pre-usage, during and post-usage.
- The emotional arousal has aspects of fantasy and operates in a multisensory way reflecting consumer self-concept consistently.
- The brand association with consumer emotions is dependent on how much fun and enjoyment is afforded by the brand.
- These feelings of pleasure constitute the 'brand experience' that consumers find memorable and desire to repeat.

In 1982 Elizabeth C. Hirschman and Morris B. Holbrook mentioned many of these already-known emotional aspects of what they called as 'hedonic consumption'. Hedonic consumption was everything that rational consumption was not. In their work, they argued that products or services that are inherently 'hedonic' in nature have more emotional involvement, tend to generate substantial mental activity (though not necessarily rational thought) and decisions regarding their consumption is based on symbolic elements rather than product features. The self-concept appeal inherent in such symbolic consumption is heavy. The information search and processing phase for a hedonic consumer is more intense. Yet, none of these aspects were being examined in existing consumer research practices by either researchers or by practitioners.

Though their work was not seminal (for very many had documented the above aspects of hedonism before they did), yet in the rebirth of truth, the Hirschman and Holbrook work is possibly seminal as it was extremely well-timed. By the early 90s the rediscovery of hedonism pioneered by them took firm hold and led scores of researchers in the US and elsewhere to examine the emotional consumer in complete earnest. Researchers involved themselves in discovering and enumerating various aesthetic and symbolic criteria that determined hedonic consumption. Hedonic research pervaded all aspects of consumption that previously had been examined only using the rational-consumer perspective–such as individual's task definition, type of involvement, search activity and personality.

The route of hedonism was experimentally used by many practitioners to emotionally connect with their consumers and several found some modicum of success in an otherwise bleak competitive situation.

Most hedonic research tended to examine luxury products and non-essentials even though theoretically everyone acknowledged that essentials were also not really being consumed for technical and functional value but had symbolic meaning for consumers. Luxury marketing and hedonic consumption came into being as special marketing courses. The hedonic consumer was more researched in the context of services. Perhaps because of the inherent higher involvement of a consumer in services across different stages, this was but natural. However, product researchers had long ago realized that all products ultimately provide a service by fulfilling the performance need – such as 'clean hair' service provided by a shampoo. Thus watches had already become service providers as time-keepers, status announcers, etc. Beauty creams were in the service business of 'providing youthfulness'.

2.3.1 Experiential Marketing in the Present Day

By the turn of the century, marketing theories (already transited from rational consumption to hedonic consumption) now moved to experiential consumption. Researchers acknowledged that for a brand it was not just about dealing with the five stages of the consumer-buying process, it was about connecting with the consumer using the five senses at every level and every moment-of-truth by providing a positive experience with the product. This experience was not purely hedonic but had significant rational components as well.

The age of the 'holistic consumer' had begun!

In their work titled *Welcome to the Experience Economy*, Pine and Gilmore clearly identify experience as a distinct offering different from products and services. In their model called 'the progression to economic value', the authors display how as a competitive position moves from undifferentiated to highly differentiated, a product moves from being a commodity to being a brand. In this transition, a commodity becomes a good, a good becomes a 'product-with-service' and a product-with-service reaches a final stage where it becomes an experience.

In other words, under highly competitive situations any offering whether product or service, is an experience. And branding an experience requires a different orientation from that of branding products and services. A consumer experience is created by focusing on stimulating consumer thoughts and emotions, is an embodiment of the brand, and all this is enabled through inspirational leadership, an empowering organizational culture and empathetic employees who are happy and fulfilled. Such planned experiences for the consumer are a source of sustainable competitive advantage, not easily replicable, revenue generating and can significantly reduce costs in the long term.

Managing consumer experiences is thus a part of management orientation within the organization and not just a question of managing consumer behaviour. The consumer is to be regarded as a part producer of the experience. All marketing decisions, of adding consumer value, communicating and delivering value, as well as new offering introductions are guided by the consumer experience salience in the entire consumption process.

2.4 *What Experiential Marketing Is Not*

The last decade has witnessed the rise of Experiential Marketing as a magic wand, as a new hope. It is a new hope but, its principles, as enumerated above, are tested and researched. We are only revisiting an existing base of knowledge with renewed rigour.

Table 1 provides a brief summation of current myths surrounding EM. It is possible that the reader may well start wondering if there is anything new about EM at all! But there is, and most assuredly! For EM is comparable to a huge palace called 'Marketing' where several 'experiential' chambers have never been stepped into. These vast chambers have always been there in the palace but they lie unexplored and somewhat unmapped too.

EM is a fairly well-researched field of inquiry. It is completely grounded in brand-consumer relationships that firmly anchor themselves in the consumer self-concept. The already existing knowledge of EM was ignored for want of attention from rational-researchers and practitioners who had much to experiment with even otherwise, and probably never needed EM before. EM is a fairly comprehensive field of inquiry. Beware the false messiahs who propagate EM as merely a communication tool or as a startling new discovery with few established principles.

Table 1: Popular myths surrounding experiential marketing

1	*EM is a new philosophy.*	EM as a philosophy has been in existence for several decades now.
2	*EM is a new marketing paradigm – it redefines marketing.*	The EM view always existed in marketing, it was never explored seriously. EM helps marketers do what they should be doing – focus on the consumer! If you call that redefining marketing...well...so be it.
3	*EM is all about consumer emotions.*	EM is about holistic view of the consumer – including both rational and emotional elements.
4	*Only EM enables a marketer to 'connect' with the consumer.*	To 'connect' with a consumer implies a Relationship Marketing (RM) orientation. RM principles have been recognized and incorporated into traditional transactional marketing for several decades now. RM has already been experimenting with consumer 'connect' for long.
5	*EM is a completely new and different methodology.*	No. These methods have been discussed, debated, recorded, used and abused by social science researchers and marketers for over a century.
6	*EM has to do with organizing events. At best it is a communication strategy execution alternative.*	That is what event management companies and advertisers would have you believe. Events continue to remain what they always were – promotional tools to be used appropriately by a marketer! EM is significantly more than just a way to execute your communication strategy.
7	*EM creates a never-ending repertoire of unforgettable and constantly delighting moments-of-truth.*	Chasing consumer 'delight' has long been abandoned as it is a nonsensical strategy in marketing. This route of constant 'delight' only increases consumer expectations and eventually leads to greater dissatisfaction and complaints. EM is not a nonsensical strategy.
8	*EM is about creativity. (It is an art and not scientific like traditional marketing.)*	Marketing has always been and continues to be, both an art and a science. The 'art' of marketing has always necessitated creativity.

9	*EM is not analytical. (It is emotional, creative.)*	No aspect of marketing is pure art. As with RM, EM also has a scientific body of knowledge (though limited in comparison) that can be consolidated and taught as a skill, subjecting EM to rational inquiry and analytical thought.
10	*EM anthropomorphizes a brand.*	There is a clear distinction between 'assigning human qualities' (personification) and 'pretending something is human' (anthropomorphism). EM helps in personifying a brand.
11	*EM methods are qualitative using focus-groups and in-depth interviews, etc.*	Partially true. However, to declare qualitative methods as superior to quantitative methods is to repeat a historical error by swinging to the other extreme. Methodology should and must always flow from the contextual information needs of a marketing decisions maker. The qualitative vs quantitative methodological divide is in itself a mythical creation.

References

1. Hirschman and Holbrook (1982), Hedonic consumption: Emerging concepts, methods and propositions, *Journal of Marketing*, 46 (Summer), 92-101
2. Holbrook and Hirschman (1982), The Experiential aspects of Consumption: Consumer Fantasies, feelings and fun, *Journal of Consumer Research*, 9 (September), 132-140
3. Holbrook "The Consumption Experience—Something New, Something Old, Something Borrowed, Something Sold"
4. Klinger, E. (1971). Structure and functions of fantasy. New York: Wiley, p 18
5. Pine and Gilmore (1998), Welcome to the Experience Economy, *Harvard Business Review*, 76 (July/August), 97-105
6. Schembri, Sharon (2006), Rationalizing service logic, or understanding services as experiences?, *Marketing Theory* 6 (3), 381-392

7. Atlas Cycles Vintage poster: http://8ate.blogspot.com/2009/06/atlas-bicycles-vintage-poster.html
8. Pears: http://www.flickr.com/photos/8592508@N04/2498955695/in/set-72157600517074635/
9. Taj Mahal, Ponds, Rallifan and Surf: http://8ate.blogspot.com/2008/04/vintage-indian-print-ads-index.html
10. Promise: http://8ate.blogspot.com/2008/09/dental-cream-vintage-ad.html
11. Emami:http://8ate.blogspot.com/2008/09/vintage-beauty-cream-advertisement.html
12. Prince Blade: http://8ate.blogspot.com/2008/05/silver-prince-tainless-blade.html
13. Rexona: http://8ate.blogspot.com/2008/09/vintage-sabun-ads.html.
14. Aesthetic Appeal Usage for Atlas Cycles: http://adsoftheworld.com/media/print/atlas_cycles_sand
15. Humour Appeal Usage for International Literacy Day: http://3.bp.blogspot.com/_jz6MAv72hK0/SrSmVRwbe2I/AAAAAAAABlY/2WNyajExqqM/s1600-h/saksharta-abhiyan-international-literacy-day.jpg

3 Understanding the Experiential Consumer

Like all of marketing should be, EM is also oriented to building a relationship with the consumer. Relationship marketing (RM) has long been accepted as the new premise by which marketers operate in an increasingly competitive environment. Several EM proponents have failed to clearly enunciate the association between EM and RM, but any position to the contrary is not tenable. If experiences are not oriented to developing better and more meaningful relationships with consumers, then EM is purposeless. If a marketer were to create an experience just for the sake of it, then it is neither strategically meaningful nor will it be adequately guided in its operational execution. EM seeks to build and maintain meaningful experiences that promote and enhance brand-consumer relationships.

Thus, in understanding the experiential consumer, one is inherently describing the relational consumer and why a relational consumer seeks experiences. This section describes how relationships form, develop, sustain and dissolve. In this section we discuss why and how people perceive brands as relational others and tend to personify brands.

The role of experiences in this relationship formation and development process is ubiquitous. The specific nature of experiences and scope of EM is detailed in the next chapter. This chapter provides the necessary insight into consumer behaviour by describing how and why individuals embed consumption experiences with relational meaning and seek self-image congruity with brands in relational terms.

3.1 Understanding Consumer Self-Concept

From the experiential marketing perspective a consumer is perceived as an individual human being performing a consumption role. This perspective is a critical departure from traditional views which invariably link a consumer with an offering. A traditional marketer would find it impossible to define a consumer unless the offering is specified. However, the experiential view firmly anchors a consumer as an individual who seeks certain relationships and experiences through consumption. Once this key perspective to a consumer is understood, a marketer is naturally keen to understand the individual human being who is carrying out the consumption roles. One key aspect to understanding individuals is their personality. Marketers have often examined consumer personality (or the self-concept) and found it correlates highly with brand personality.

3.1.1 Self-Concept, Identities and Individual Values

Self-concept is best understood as an overall perception about the self that an individual has developed about himself. It is a kind of self-reference point which the individual uses to interact with the whole world. This reference point helps an individual separate good from bad, decide upon right from wrong, perceive differences subjectively between nice and un-nice and decide what is desirable and what is not. These judgments of the individual apply universally – to himself as well as to all people and all objects including brands. Understanding the consumer self-concept enables marketers to understand how an individual sees himself/herself and uses such knowledge to guide behaviour, especially in developing brand attitudes and for sustaining beliefs towards brand personalities.

The self-concept is a complex multidimensional construct. But it can be broadly sub-divided into two distinct though interrelated components: the personal identity and the social identity.

The Personal Identity: Personal identity refers to how one sees oneself as an individual. The personal identity consists of all those thoughts, feelings and impressions that an individual possesses about one's own traits, interests, values, and attitudes. The personal identity keeps a person believing that he or she is a unique individual in this whole wide world. It is through the personal identity that an individual differentiates oneself from all other individuals. The personal identity is a measure of the sense of individualism in a person. Imagine for a moment that you are picking small pebbles from a potful of rice in a closed cabin. There is another person in the next cabin doing the same mundane unskilled task. The cabin is closed, so you cannot see the other person. You cannot make out if that person is an Indian or not, a man or a woman, a child or an adult, an educated professional or a wayward alcoholic. In other words, you have no 'social' anchors or cues to create any stereotype or image of the other person. If you converse with this other person, it would be based purely on your 'personal identity' – your sense of individualized uniqueness.

Personal identity is what makes a person feel unique even within a social group where there is a sense of belonging. The personal identity is what makes a person feel unique even in a group of like-minded people. For example, even though I am just one amongst trillion authors past and present, I think of myself as possessing a unique mix of eccentricities and traits that make me different from all others authors of this world. That special mix as I perceive it constitutes my personal identity. You think of yourself as a unique individual different from all other million readers of this book. That special mix, as you perceive it, is your personal identity.

Another way to understand the personal identity is to think of it as an individual's character. When we say 'This person has a weak character', we are usually referring to a poorly formed personal identity and weak related values.

The Social Identity: The social identity refers to how one sees oneself as part of some social group(s). Social identity comes from a sense of belonging to a group. Individuals naturally have multiple social identities based on the number of social identity 'in-groups' that one has membership of. These group identities can be involuntary where the individual has no choice (such as gender, income, race, age) or those to which one belongs by choice (such as voluntarily choosing one's political and sexual preferences). There are numerous dimensions of social identity construction. In India, regional and language-based social identities are strong affiliations for consumers that influence consumption patterns and brand perceptions significantly. Social identities also are constructed based on your address – living in the town area of Mumbai has different implications for the social identity as compared to living in the suburbs. Usually, social identity 'in-groups' are considered by an individual as superior to all other 'out-groups'. An individual tends to think more positively about one's own in-groups. Thus by belonging to a certain region with a certain 'mother-tongue' makes one think of the in-group-all those who speak the same language, as somewhat culturally superior to other out-groups – all those who do not speak that language.

When the self is perceived in terms of one's social identity, the norms, attitudes, and behaviours of the relevant social in-group define and guide the self-concept. Let us assume for example that all professors are vague and pedantic and accept others as part their in-group based on how quaintly vague and eccentrically pedantic they are. I am a professor in an academic institution. I choose to act vague and pedantic, so I can be part of the in-group I want to be considered a part of.

On the other hand, I may choose otherwise. Social identity groups need not imply conformity. An individual could identify himself as part of an in-group but still act as a non-conformist with the group propagated attitudes and behaviour. I am a professor who is not vague and pedantic. I choose to not conform to the social identity group norms that I am a part of. In doing so, I exercise my personal identity over this social group. Rebels in social identity groups are common. Teenagers who are exploring their personal identities often act as 'rebels without a cause' within their family social identity groups. It is also possible that another social identity weighs heavily. For example, a teenager identifies strongly with the social group of friends who colour their hair green and wear jeans that are torn in exactly five places. This friends-social identity may bear heavily and cause the person to stress those group norms even within the family in-group where norms of behaviour are drastically different. In other words, the social identity associations with 'rebellious and irreverent friends' is so important to the self-concept that it is exercised even with the family (which is a different social in-group with distinctly different norms).

Non-conformance to social identity norms will necessarily result in some friction due to identity conflicts. Minor identity conflicts are quite normal and are usually resolved through focus on the 'hierarchy'. Hierarchy refers to the ranking of social identities in an individual's mind. Identities naturally occupy hierarchical positions in an individual's self-concept. One individual may be more conscious of the personal identity while another individual may operate largely from the social identity domain. Even the social identities are arranged in some hierarchical order. This is not a 'global hierarchy' (meaning a fixed hierarchy which is operating consistently at all times and in all contexts). Hierarchy is always dependent on the context in which the individual operates. When I am shopping alone and for myself, the personal identity is predominant. When I am eating out with family the family-social identity takes precedence, when with colleagues, it is the workplace social identity. Depending on the construction of the self-concept and the situational factors, the 'salient' social identity varies. I am at a mall with my family busy being noisy and having immense silly fun when I meet my pompous boss. I immediately straighten up and adopt a more suitable behaviour which is appropriate as per my workplace social identity norms. Or I wave my hand at my boss and continue behaving like a kid (giving greater hierarchical level to my family-based social identity). The choice of hierarchy in any situation depends on how an individual decodes the situational context, the strength of each social identity and the values of the individual.

3.1.2 Self-Concept and Values

Values refer to basic convictions of an individual. These convictions determine what an individual considers as desirable actions and state-of-being. Based on values, an individual arrives at judgements of what to choose and what to reject. Values are strongly linked with the self-concept, determining and being determined by both personal and social preferences. Values underlie all attitudinal processes that influence an individual's choices.

Values held by (the majority in) a group are also called as 'group norms' which are socio-culturally determined (though usually norms are related largely to how one should behave rather than how one should think and feel). Values and norms are considered as the 'drivers' that respectively distinguish one individual from another and one social 'in-group' from the 'out-groups'.

Since the strongest social identities are often involuntary (memberships such as gender-based, family-based, religion-based on which family one is born into, etc.) the influence of social identities on values is strong. To the extent that life experiences influence values, a sense of the personal identity determines the values an individual holds.

Values, personal or social, of an individual can also be distinguished based on the 'current' and the 'desirable' where desirable values are what individuals aspire for as admirable and good. Desirable values determine what social groups an individual aspires for and also contribute to the individual sense of personal identity. But it is the current values that relate to day-to-day life and have a greater influence on individual behaviour in the present. The desirable values relate to ideological issues and play a limited role in common interpersonal interaction for most individuals.

Figure 3.1: The consumer self-concept, identities and selves

		Actual self	**Ideal self**
	Description	Current values possessed by the individual	Desirable values (not possessed currently but aspired for)
Personal identity	What makes me unique as an individual and how that uniqueness builds my self-esteem		
Social identities	What groups I belong to and how that sense of belonging builds my self-esteem		

This classification in values associates individual to two kinds of selves – the actual self and the ideal self.

Figure 3.2 has some examples of brand positions where I believe that brand personality implications were not judged. It is possible that in these ads the strategic communication objective was never to convey any brand personality at all. Yet consumers do and will always perceive a brand as saying something to them (especially if the creativity grabs their attention as in case of each of these wonderfully creative ads I have cited as examples) – and what is being said by the brand will be judged by consumers based on their own self-concept. Some of these ads I believe are likely to even have a negative effect on some consumer self-concepts. The first in ad Figure 3.2 is of a large convenience food brand. It is a beautifully creative ad, but who is the brand talking to? Is the ad addressing women who are responsible for cooking for the family and enjoy that social identity, or is it targeted at the personal identity of single women who would like to focus on their careers, or is it talking to feminists who would probably want to question why cooking is in the domain of a woman at all! What the ad represents to me is what women have not achieved in comparison to men. The gender-based social identity of women is being challenged in this ad. How many women would like a brand personality that challenges their social identity based on gender? How many women would feel connected with a brand which makes them feel defensive? How appropriate is this brand personality positioning especially in the Indian context?

I spoke to nearly twenty women belonging to SEC A in Mumbai and Ahmedabad about the concept embedded in the third ad in Figure 3.2 (without revealing the brand). Most were bemused though some were a little miffed about being depicted as a goat-headed person. Several of the working women told me that when they reach home and cook something and their husbands return, the smell of food reassured the husband that dinner was at home and/or that the wife was in a good mood. Other women felt that their husbands and children liked to guess what had been cooked based on how she and the house smelt when they returned from work or play. This 'guessing' was a family togetherness activity that occurred almost as a daily ritual. The consumption situation inherent in the cooking process marks the smell of food cooking as a significant positive symbol for family-social identity. The operating consumer social identities are not attracted by the brand promise to make the house insipidly smell-free. The brand will not be able to construct a meaningful relationship with such consumers using this route.

Figure 3.2: Association between brand personality and consumer self

	A convenience food ad. The line states: 'If only women spent less time cooking'.
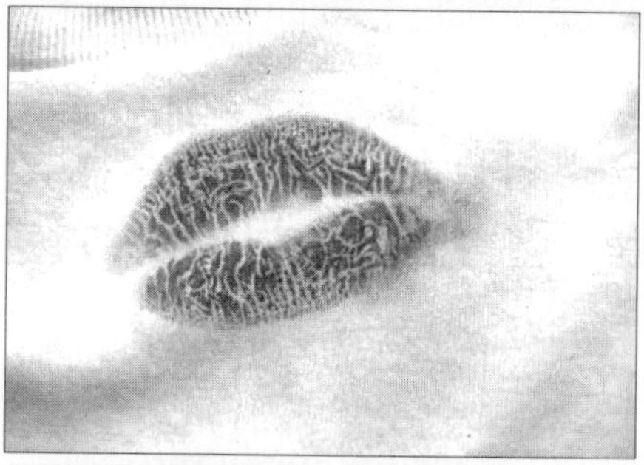	A detergent ad: The adline states: 'No 'stains, no stories'.
	A kitchen ventilation system ad: The adline states: 'Do you smell like the food you cook?'

The second ad for a detergent powder I can only refer to as mischievous if not devious in its positioning. The brand personality promises to keep your secrets confidential. But what secrets kept from whom? And who is the brand talking to? Is it targeted at men encouraging them to quietly wash up their clothes and remove tell-tale signs? If so, then the brand personality is well-created. If it is speaking to women, then I am not sure how the brand expects to be considered positively by women in their social identity roles as cherished wives and mothers.

The association between the self and the identity determines what reference point is used by an individual to assess a brand. Broad consumer concerns are depicted in Figure 3.3 for each identity and operating self.

Figure 3.3: The consumer self-concept, identities and selves

		Actual self	Ideal self
	Description	Current values possessed by the individual	Desirable values (not possessed currently but aspired for)
Personal identity	What makes me unique as an individual and how that uniqueness builds my self-esteem	Will the brand satisfy/enhance my personal identity or will it damage my personal identity?	Will the brand satisfy my aspirations about personal identity, or will it make me miserable by conflicting with my actual self-social identity? E.g. the first ad in Figure 3.2
Social identities	What groups I belong to and how that sense of belonging builds my self-esteem	Will the brand fit into my social in-groups norms or will it reduce my sense of belonging and damage my current memberships? E.g. the third ad in Figure 3.2	Will the brand help me fit into my aspirational social identity group or will I be only mocked at in my current groups? E.g. the second ad in Figure 3.2

The first ad (Figure 3.2) could be appealing to the ideal self-personal identity of a woman. But if that brand personality is in conflict with the operating actual self-social identity that is prominent in the consumption situation, the brand personality will be rejected.

When creating and communicating brand personalities, a marketer needs to understand the consumption process on the following counts:

1. What is my consumer's self-concept? What are the key values and norms for the consumer in the given consumption context.
2. Which identity is operating in the given consumption context? Is it the personal identity or is it one of the social identities? If a social identity is prominent, then which social identity is operating in that context? Why? What are those identity needs?
3. How can my brand add meaningfulness to my consumer's self-concept? Does it appeal to the actual or the ideal self:
   a. What is the nature of my offering itself? Is it inherently related to the day-to-day life of the consumer or is it inherently aspirational in nature?
   b. What is the meaning of my brand? What does it stand for? Will the consumer 'like' my brand or will he 'respect and admire' it – i.e. will it appeal to his actual or his ideal self?
4. Does my brand personality stand for something significant that my consumer will notice and appreciate?
5. Does my brand personality threaten the consumer self-concept in any way ? Will my brand personality feel like an elusive mirage and frustrate my consumer? Will my brand seem like any other common-man with really nothing special about it to make it seem interesting?

3.1.3 Consumer Self-Concept and Congruity

To answer the above questions, a marketer needs to make informed judgements about the extent of 'congruity' between the brand personality and the consumer self-concept. Congruity refers to the degree to which an individual (whether part of ad audience, a shopper at a store or a consumer of any offering at any stage of decision-making) finds a meaningful association between own self-concept and the brand personality. This association need not always be in terms of 'similarity', it often takes on hues of complementarity. For example, a soft-spoken consumer may admire and respect a flashy and 'powerful' brand rather than prefer a soft-spoken elegant brand.

Consumers 'seek' congruity in relationships with brands because it contributes to their own self-concept in a positive way. Congruity evaluations consequently are a means to achieve 'meaningfulness' in relationships for enhancing own self-concept. Congruity is not a goal in itself.

The strong association between consumer ownership of a brand and perceived congruity between self-concept and brand-personality has been almost universally evidenced across a wide variety of products and across different cultural settings. To be able to identify and manipulate the elements that contribute to congruity, the congruity process of relationship development needs to be understood by a marketer.

3.2 Value-Congruity in Brand-Consumer Relationships

As already stated, any individual's primary needs are simply to sustain and enhance both the components of the self-concept – i.e. the personal identity and the social identity. The development and sustenance of the self-concept is managed, to a large extent, through relationships forged with others. Relationships with family and friends and workplace colleagues help define and sustain our self-concepts. We choose friends who are chilled-out or ambitious, simple or complicated, fun-loving or philosophical based on how we see ourselves. Our values and interests shape our choice of relationships and the nature/quality of our relationships. Similarly consumers form relationships with brands because it contributes to maintaining and enhancing the self-concept of the consumer.

Extensive research has established the fact that consumers develop relationships with brands based on the same processes and relational elements that determine their interpersonal relationships. Individuals who regard themselves in a particular way evaluate others (people and brands) on similar value yardsticks. If honesty is important to me (whatever I define as 'honesty' for myself), I assess others based on how similarly honest they are. This process applies equally to objects and brands that come my way as it applies with people I meet. Susan Fournier has several detailed works on why and how people regularly use processes such as 'animism' to personify objects. The purpose is to have meaningful relationships with brands so as to give greater meaning to own self-concept. This personification of a brand is a natural and an inherent tendency with human beings because it helps create meaning around whatever they perceive and do – it gives meaning to life and living. Thus a personified brand-image is generated naturally in a brand-consumer relationship. The quality of the relationship determines the attitudes and behaviour towards that brand. If the quality of relationship is not too great, the consumer's loyalty to that brand is equally lacklustre.

What is the basis on which consumers construct this personified brand image? Research evidence shows that in initial stages an impression of the brand is created based on how similar the brand appears to the consumer's own self-concept in terms of trustworthiness. Initial evaluations by adults of other people and brands is based on how much the other can be trusted. In assessing this, individuals use the yardstick of their own values as the reference point. The reference points keep changing as the relationship progresses. This progression of relationships using values and identities as the reference point is the basic premise of the Value-Congruity Relationship Theory.

3.3 The Value-Congruity Relationship Theory

The Value-Congruity Relationship Theory posits that brand-consumer relationship progression depends on the extent to which the values of individuals are congruous with the perceived brand values. The greater the value-congruity, greater is the relationship quality. This theory provides a powerful explanation for how brand-consumer relationships develop, delineating specific developmental stages. The theory provides a road-map for a marketer on a) how to construct brand personalities and b) how and when to modify the personality to enhance the relationship quality.

The central tenets of the Value-Congruity Relationship Theory are that:

1. Social norms and personal values that are embedded in an individual's self-concept are the primary drivers of all human action including building relationships.
2. Relationships satisfy inherent self-concept needs of individuals. The desire to form meaningful relationships with brands is natural. This causes people to search for brand persona and interpret all communications from that perspective, even if a firm does not mean to create a brand persona for itself.
3. Subject to their relational needs and dispositions to invest in new relationships, people choose when and how their relationships will progress based on their norms and values.
4. Extent of harmony between self-concept and the brand personality determines extent of congruity.
5. Level of perceived congruity determines the quality of brand-consumer relationship.

6. Relationships with greater quality and strength progress into intense relationships that are enduring and sustaining.

Figure 3.4: Circles of meaningfulness: Classifying relationships on the basis of form

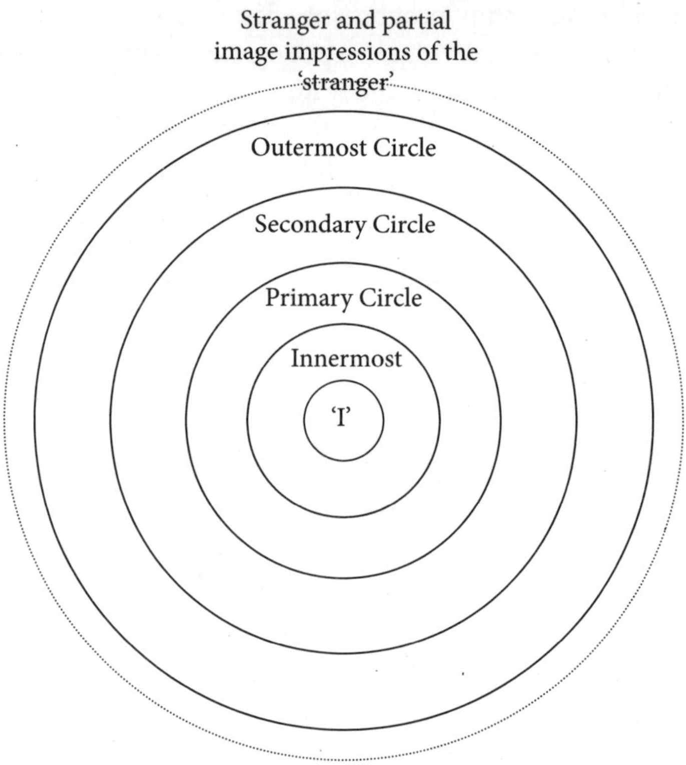

This theory envisages all relationships of an individual, whether with other people or with brands, as falling in concentric circles around the individual (see Figure 3.4). Farthest from the individual are strangers/acquaintances and closest are those people and brands that give intense meaning to the individual's self-concept. In the closest – 'Innermost' – circle, exist those people with whom the relationship helps define the self.

Relationships are classified by an individual and each category (circle) is treated differently by applying different interpersonal rules. Because of this encircled view, relationships do not really 'progress' except within the same circle. Across the circles, relationships change form where the 'other' is no longer perceived to be the 'same person'.

Progression in relationships is not a natural outcome in the process of relationship formation. It is a conscious decision an individual makes to change a relationship form into another higher-order form.

Understanding the broad stages in relationship formation and development will help a marketer understand consumer needs at various stages and plan the brand experience accordingly.

Stage One: Strangers, the start-point of our theory, are those about whom an individual possesses no (meaningful) information (Figure 3.5). The movement from being a stranger to being a 'desirable' relationship partner starts when an individual forms a positive impression of the other and desires (further) interaction. These impressions can form even without any interaction on the basis of credence-based cues interpreted symbolically (for instance the other's observed appearance used to make attributions about personality). Such credence-based initial impressions are not necessarily weak. They can be intense (you sometimes like or dislike a person upon sight). However, the relationship itself is rather fragile and needs efforts. At this stage the primary effort to be made by the marketer is simply to provide the right symbolic cues and plenty of symbolic cues for consumer to indulge in observing and judging.

In the context of a brand, the initial cues which a consumer uses to arrive at initial impressions emerge from brand advertisements, perceived brand reputation, word-of-mouth impressions, informal discussion with various social identity groups, newspaper articles, fliers, inserts, brand point-of-purchase materials and other brand tangibles that an individual sees and touches when passing through a store, etc.

Figure 3.5: Pre-relationship formation: Moving from 'stranger' to relational 'meaningfulness'

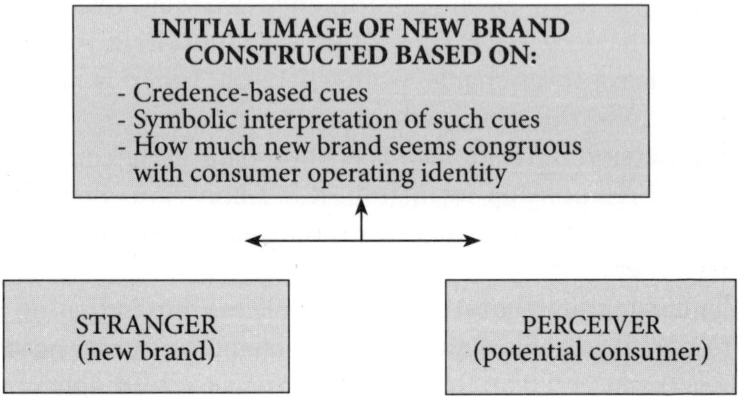

Impressions about the other can take time to form or be instantaneous depending on the nature and intensity of cues and the strength of associations an individual has with those cues. Impressions formed on 'trivial values' have no meaningfulness. Recognizing this ambiguity in impression formation, Figure 3.4 depicts a dotted circle at the outer layer. Individual propensities to take risks would significantly influence the level of interactions at this stage.

Stage Two: Based on the impressions obtained about the brand, the initial judgements of the consumer are based on two critical aspects: i) how trustworthy do I find the brand and ii) what promise does it hold for which of my 'experiential seeks'. Trust is the basic foundation of relationships. It is to a certain extent a socially embedded instinct. You trust a stranger walking on the road to not abuse you verbally or physically. Without such socially and instinctively placed trust, any adult would end up being dysfunctionally paranoid.

Figure 3.6: First stage in relationship formation: Trusted image leading to consumer desire to interact

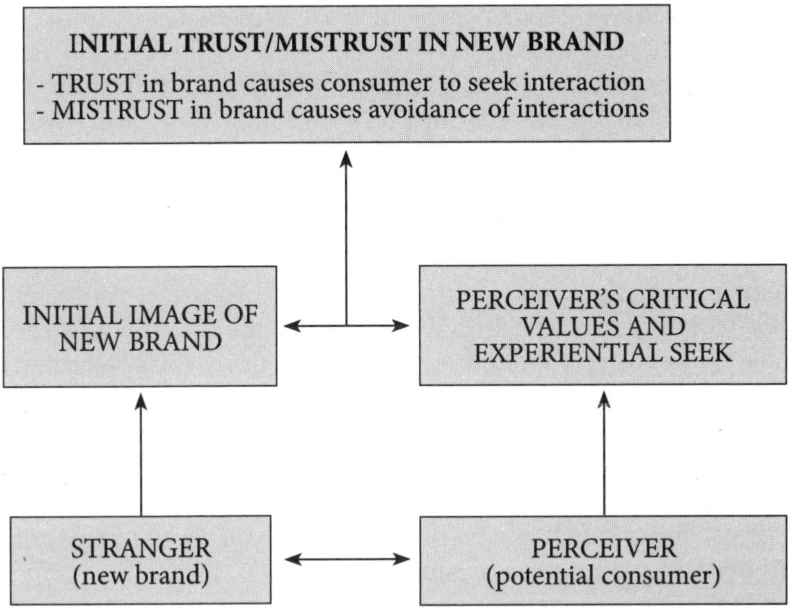

Over and above this socially engendered trust, individuals have their own unique thresholds of trust. Some of us are happy cynics, trusting people only with much interaction. Others amongst us are more predisposed to trust people, having what is generally called a 'more trusting nature'. Depending on this individual 'propensity to trust' and how the new brand persona addresses the trustfulness needs, a consumer will trust or mistrust the brand. This is depicted in Figure 3.6 as the initial image leading to a person to trust and thereby seek experiential interactions. 'Experiential seek' refers to what experiences the individual consumer is associating with the brand based on initial impressions. The initial brand impressions need to be managed to convey appropriate experiential promises. The concept of Experiential seek is described in greater detail in the next chapter.

Once initial trust is placed in the brand and the experiential platform of the brand has been assessed, the consumer either decides to seek further interactions or run away! If your brand does not address key concerns of trust or does not promise an experiential seek that appeals to consumers, there is no need for them to waste their time. Time is precious and there are too many trustworthy brands out there that hold more worthwhile experiential promises. However, if the consumer finds the brand worthy of basic trust and perceives an appealing experiential promise, interactions with the brand are actively sought. Too often brands begin to communicate with the consumers without ensuring sufficient interaction points. In today's age, people will seek to interact at the initial stages through channels of their choice, not yours. Remember, that at this stage, the consumer is not completely decided, even if you are sure you want to get into a steady relationship. Some consumers will hit the website, some will hunt for you in their favourite newspaper, others will want to visit you personally at your nearest outlet and merely interact without doing much or any business with you. Often firms miss out on using the power of multiple channels. Multiple channels are a fact of life today though little is known about how they can be best managed.

Stage Three: Once the interaction occurs, two key processes kick into place (Figure 3.7):

i) the process of confirmation and disconfirmation of credence-based cues: Confirmation and disconfirmation refers to adjustments the consumer makes in his or her initial perceptions. 'I thought the store would be swankier than it what it seemed in the ad, it is not so elegant as I thought it would be.' Or 'I thought this restaurant would be efficient from how my friend spoke about it, it is quite laid-back.' There can also be a confirmation of initial impressions such as 'Hey! I did expect this store to be informal but I never thought they would be so cheerful and friendly!'

ii) the added evaluation and assessment based on further experiential cues observed and gathered during the interaction. These cues are gathered during active interaction with the brand and by seeing the brand in action. As with people, judgements based on seeing a brand-in-action are more intense because impressions are now backed by personally gathered evidence.

Figure 3.7: Second stage in relationship formation: Interactions leading to clearer brand-consumer congruity assessments

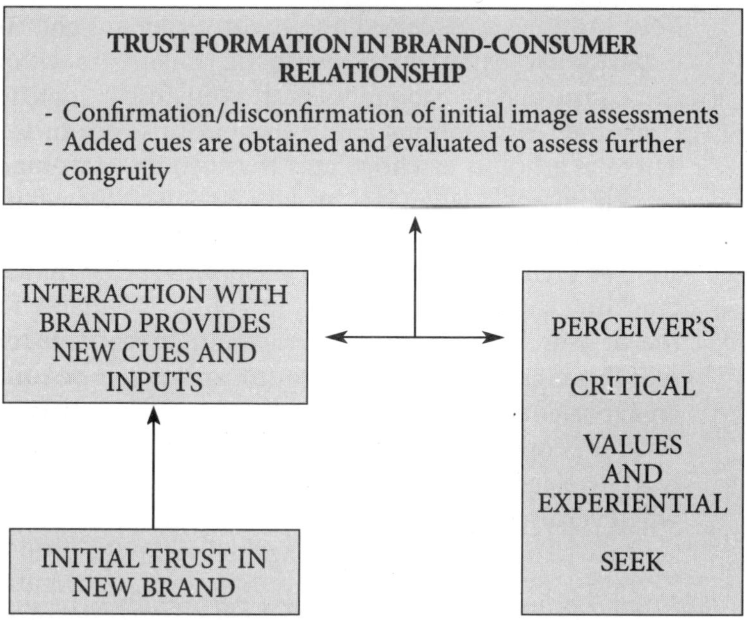

The resultant brand personality post-interactions is less fragile than the credence-cue based initial impressions created through stages one and two. The platform for a relationship (or lack of it) is usually set at this stage.

Marketers need to manage the third stage in a brand-consumer relationship by keeping in mind the following issues:

I. *Ensure trust-related cues are supplemented in the initial interaction:* If your communications positioned your shirt as an 'honest' shirt priced at Rs200 onwards, ensure that your store has sufficient stocks starting Rs200 onwards. I have often seen such claims advertised by various brands of shirts with great fanfare but upon a store visit I was told that the Rs200 – Rs350 range shirts are out of stock. These brands I have since considered as rather dishonest persona ever since. Their subsequent similar claims have no credibility with me. I just dismiss them summarily.

II. *Ensure experiential seek is fulfilled in the initial interaction:* Your brand was perceived by the consumer as promising a particular experiential platform. Ensure that when the consumer first interacts with your brand, the basic consumer expectations about that promise are fulfilled. There is a brand of chocolates that promises a crunchy crackling 'krick' when it is broken into two pieces before being eaten. When I bought the brand and opened it as soon as I reached home, it was sticky and soft. It made no crackling sound but literally went 'phut'. Whenever I see the ad now, I have a bit of a natural shield which tells me that this is advertising exaggeration and not to be read as an experiential promise. We all have such shields against several people whom we have met in life – people who tend to exaggerate about themselves. We naturally reduce whatever they are saying by a certain delta quantity. Not the way to build the best of relationships, right?

III. *Additional promises about the brand personality:* The initial interaction provides a multitude of cues to a consumer by which the initial brand perceptions are enriched and a more complete brand personality is seen. Marketers most often tend to over-promise at this stage. There is another conceptual issue I have with conveying all promises at this stage. If everything about you is laid open at our very first meeting, I have nothing further to discover about you. The most beautiful and lasting relationships are those that take a little time and plenty of continuously desired interactions. They are not based on how much you know the other person, but instead are based on how much you *desire* to know the other person. There is an excellent skin clinic brand which makes an immense effort to manage initial interactions. When a consumer visits them for the first time, they are greeted very nicely, invited to sit in expansive comfortable chairs in a soothing and reassuring ambience, served a yummy, healthy drink and the doctor comes out to the reception area and invites the consumer in by calling them by their names. This process is wonderfully executed, each and every time the consumer comes and visits them, whether a new consumer or a loyal one. If one were to take the relational route, then some of these executions I would have suggested should be deferred. A doctor coming out and inviting the person in by name would feel so special to the consumer if it happened on the third or fourth visit. The consumer would feel special and remembered. Currently, the process right from start has disabled any possibility of relational progression using this particular cue. All one has done is to convey to the consumer that this is your caring rule book procedure – nothing specially for you as an individual consumer because you are loyal and you keep coming back to us.

At this stage and onwards, the consumer has two sets of cues to evaluate – the credence-based cues from ads and other symbolic inputs, and the experience-based cues that come from an evaluation of actual performance in terms of brand reliability. Both these cues are interpreted and experience from each is transferred to assess further value-congruity perceptions. Somewhere in this stage, emotions start playing a key role. Functional experience is by and large assured, now the consumer will explore if the brand can mean something more than just an 'acquaintance'. The consumer will now start checking out your brand to see if your brand can become a 'friend'. Emotions start playing a key role besides the initial rational and cognitive evaluations. Figure 3.8 indicates how a relationship progresses from initial-image formation to trust (and desire for interaction) to desire to have higher order emotional need fulfilment.

At this stage a consumer moves beyond just the 'Critical' values and brings in all 'prominent' values to the brand personality wanting to know how much the brand complements these 'Prominent' values as well. Prominent values are not necessary for a relationship to exist, but they are necessary for a relationship to develop further. We all meet people who we classify as 'nice' and 'trustworthy' but they remain as good acquaintances. They never progress to being friends because though our critical values match, the other 'nice-to-have' values do not match. Our interests, view of life, etc. differ so much that the relationship somehow never moves to a higher place. Brand-consumer relationships tend to get stuck similarly when brands fail to address the additional values that are prominently part of an individual's experiential seek and operating identity.

Figure 3.8: Relational enhancement – moving to the primary circle

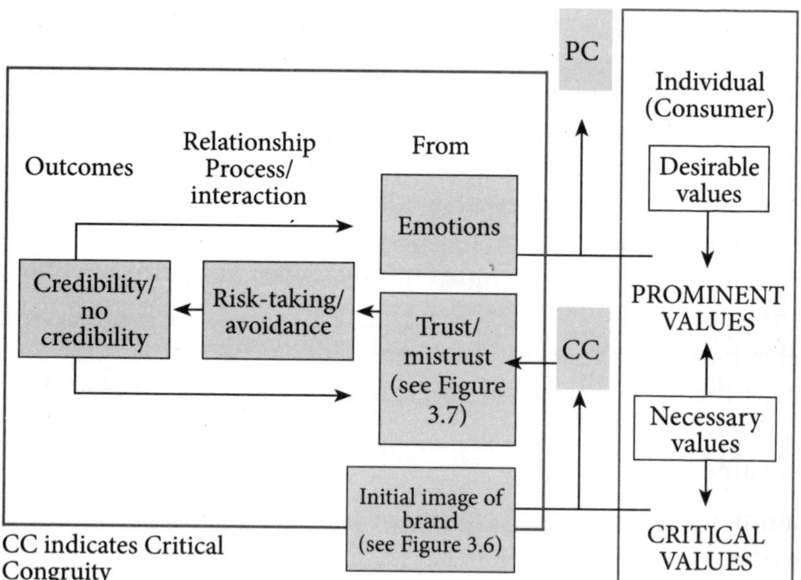

CC indicates Critical Congruity
PC indicates Prominent Congruity

Stage Four: Once the emotional expectations are unlocked, the relationship becomes exceedingly rich and continuously changes in form and intensity. Figure 3.9 depicts how at different stages, different sets of values are important for ensuring brand-consumer congruity and hence relational progression.

Figure 3.9: Association between value-congruity and relationship

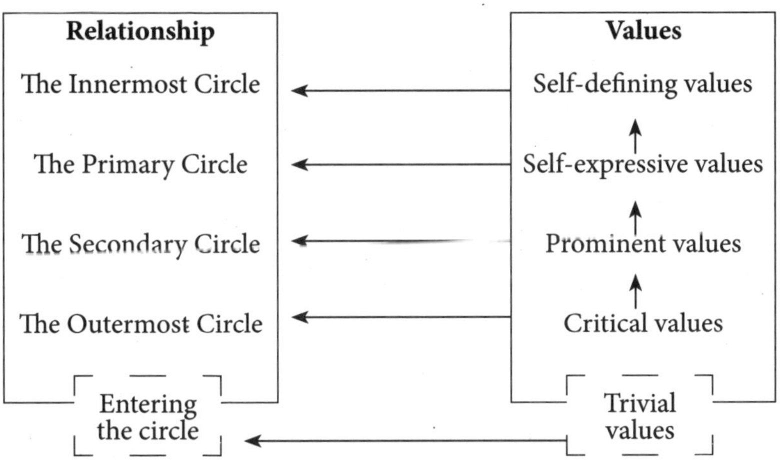

Any brand needs to first cross the threshold of 'critical congruity' and be assured that consumer base expectations will be fulfilled. Subsequently, 'doing more of the same' is wasteful and even dangerous at times. Brands need to move to higher-order stages, analytically sourcing and employing consumer behaviour insights and then creatively addressing consumer needs through experiential marketing. The aim of experiential marketing should be always to maintain and enhance the brand-consumer relationship.

Comparing the VCR Model of Relationships with other Existing Models

Relationship are formed and operate as open systems. Open systems are heavily interrelated, with many networks, and have a plethora of variables that a marketer needs to understand and address. However, this chapter provides a usable relationship formation and progression theory that enables experiential marketers to plan and guide their experiential efforts. In achieving this, a clear specification of the consumer identities and identity-related needs is sufficient for explaining variations in relationship formation as well as relationship outcomes.

The proposed Value-Congruity Relationship is developed keeping in mind 'free choice' – the shopper is free to choose which brand to build a relationship with. Yet this VCR Model is capable of explaining not just the formation of relationships right from the stage of initiation, but through the identity associations, the model also has the ability to explain relationships and interactions that one does not/cannot choose such as family ties, etc. that are in some way restricted in choice.

VCR model takes into account consumer behaviour as well as underlying attitudes and provides explanations for both. Unlike existing congruity models, this focus on values and identities along with behaviour makes this model extremely useful for marketers. Unlike existing multi-attribute models, the Value Congruity Relationship Model accounts for consumer experiences and emotions. It does not consider consumer behaviour as merely an outcome of rational and cognitive evaluations of brand performance across specific brand attributes.

> The self-concept of any individual comprises the personal identity and several social identities. The personal identity provides a sense of uniqueness to the individual and the social identities aid in maintaining and enhancing the self-concept by an emphasis on 'in-group-out-group' differences that are usually biased in favour of the in-group. Individuals feel a constant and inherent need to maintain a positive esteem for their self-concept. All behaviour is motivated to achieve this goal. Thus, people consume brands and visit stores that help develop and enhance their self-concept.

References

1. Aaker, Jennifer L. (1999) The Malleable Self: The Role of Self-Expression in Persuasion, *Journal of Marketing Research*, 36 (1), 45-57
2. Ackerman and Tellis (2001) Can Culture affect prices? A cross-cultural study of shopping and retail prices, *Journal of Retailing*, 77 (1), 12-14
3. Ashkanasy and O'Connor (1997) Value Congruence in Leader-Member Exchange, *Journal of Social Psychology*, 137 (5), 647-662
4. Barone, Shimp and Sprott (1999) The Mere-Ownership Effect: 'More There Than Meets Their Eyes' or 'Less There Than They Would Have Us Believe'?, *Journal of Consumer Psychology*, 6 (3), 299-311
5. Belk, R.W. (1975) Situational Variables in Consumer Behaviour, *Journal of Consumer Research*, 2 (December), 157-164
6. Bharadwaj and Menon (1993) Determinants of Success in Service Industries, *Journal of Services Marketing*, 7 (4), 19-40
7. Bharadwaj, Sundar G.; Varadarajan, P. Rajan and Fahy, John (1993) Sustainable competitive advantage in service industries: A Conceptual Model and Research Propositions, *Journal of Marketing*, 57 (October). 83-99
8. Birdwell Al E. (1968) Automobiles and Self-Imagery: Reply, *Journal of Business*, 41 (4), 486-487
9. Cheung, Siu-Kau (1997) Self-discrepancy and Depressive Experiences among Chinese Early Adolescents: Significance of Identity and the Undesired Self, *International Journal of Psychology*, 32 (5), 347
10. Devine, F. (1992), Social identities, class identities and political perspectives, *Sociological Review*, 40 (2), 229-253
11. Fajer, Mary and Schouten, John (1995) Breakdown and Dissolution of Person-Brand Relationships, *Advances in Consumer Research*, 22 (1), 663-667
12. Fournier Susan (1995) Toward the Development of Relationship Theory at the Level of the Product and Brand, *Advances in Consumer Research*, 22 (1), 661-662

13. Fournier Susan (1998) Consumers and Their Brands: Developing Relationship Theory in Consumer Research, *Journal of Consumer Research*, 24 (4), 343-373
14. Frazier, Spekman, and O'Neal (1988) Just-In-Time Exchange Relationships in Industrial Markets, *Journal of Marketing*, 52 (October), 52-67
15. Graen and Schiemann (1978) Leader-Member Agreement: A Vertical Dyad Linkage Approach, *Journal of Applied Psychology*, 63 (April), 206-212
16. Hem, Leif E. and Iversen, Nina M. (2002) Decomposed Similarity Measures in Brand Extensions, *Advances in Consumer Research*, 29 (1), 199-206
17. Hofstede, Geert (1980) Culture and Organizations, *International Studies of Management & Organization*, 10 (Winter), 15-41
18. Hogg, Margaret K.; Cox, Alastair J. and Keeling, Kathy (2000) The impact of self-monitoring on image congruence and product/ brand evaluation, *European Journal of Marketing*, 34 (5/6), 641-666
19. Hughes, G. David and Guerrero, Jose L. (1971) "Automobile Self-Congruity Models Reexamined," *Journal of Marketing Research*, 8 (February): 125-127
20. Jones, Gareth R. and George, Jennifer M. (1998). "The Experience And Evolution Of Trust: Implications for Cooperation and Teamwork," *Academy of Management Review*, 23 (July), 531-546
21. Kamp, Edward and MacInnis, Deborah J. (1995) Characteristics of portrayed emotions in commercials: When does what is shown in ads affect viewers?, *Journal of Advertising Research*, 35 (November/December): 19-28
22. Kirmani, Amna and Shiv, Baba (1998) Effects of Source Congruity on Brand Attitudes and Beliefs: The Moderating Role of Issue-Relevant Elaboration, *Journal of Consumer Psychology*, 7 (1), 25-47
23. Kleine, Robert E. III; Kleine, Susan Schultz and Kernan, Jerome B. (1993) Mundane Consumption and the Self: A social-Identity Perspective, *Journal of Consumer Psychology*, 2 (3), 209-253

24. Komiak, Sherrie Y. X.; Weiquan Wang; Benbasat, Izak (2005) Trust Building in Virtual Salespersons Versus in Human Salespersons: Similarities and Differences, *e-Service Journal*, 3 (Summer). 49-63
25. Lantz, Garold and Loeb, Sandra (1998) An examination of the community identity and purchase preferences using the social identity approach, *Advances in Consumer Research*, 25 (1), 486-491
26. Robbins S.P. (2001) Organizational Behavior (9th ed.), New Jersey: Prentice-Hall.
27. Schlenker, Barry R. (1978) Attitudes As Actions: Social Identity Theory And Consumer Research, *Advances in Consumer Research*, 5 (1), 352-359
28. Tam, Sing-Fai; Chan, Mei Hing; Lam, Hoi Wa and Lam, Lai Hing (2003) Comparing the Self-Concepts of Hong Kong Chinese Adults With Visible and Not Visible Physical Disability, *Journal of Psychology*, 137 (4), 363-372
29. Verlegh, Peeter W.J. (1999) Ingroups, Outgroups and Stereotyping: Consumer Behaviour and Social Identity Theory, *Advances in Consumer Research*, 26, 162-169

4 Scope and Nature of Experiential Marketing

This section explains the characteristics of experiences and defines the scope and nature of Experiential Marketing (EM).

4.1 What Are Experiences?

The Merriam-Webster dictionary defines Experience as the 'conscious events that make up an individual life; something personally encountered, undergone, or lived through; the act or process of directly perceiving events or reality'. In EM we define consumer experience as the internal and subjective response consumers have to any and all direct and indirect contacts with an offering as perceived by the consumer. Direct contact occurs when the consumer buys, handles or uses the offering, sees the ad campaign or reads an advertorial. Indirect contact happens when the consumer interacts with indirect representations of the brand – such as word-of-mouth of another consumer, published reviews and articles, etc., or passes by a billboard containing the company logo which he associates with the brand which is not part of the offering per se. The latter and several elements in the former are often beyond direct control of the firm.

Consumer experience refers to the totality of all contacts (direct and indirect) till date. In EM experiences are not a one-time event. Research indicates that though most recent events and contacts have greater salience in defining overall experience. However, the totality of past experiences tempers consumer judgments and perceptions.

4.2 Assessing Experiences

Experiences, by their very nature, are too complex to be enumerated as comprising any 'list' of elements. The attractiveness of EM is precisely because experiences embody the whole set of direct and indirect interactions between a brand and a consumer. However, there is a clear need to be able to assess experiences. Without any form of such measurement, no marketer would be able to figure out where the current consumption experiences stand and where and how they need to be guided in future.

In assessing experiences, it is necessary to understand the salience of experiences. Experiential Salience can broadly be explained as a combination of

$$\text{intensity of experience} \times \text{nature of experience}$$

4.2.1 Experiential Salience: Intensity of Experience

Intensity of experience can be divided into three broad component parts:

1. Which of the consumer senses are being engaged, for how long and what is the consumer impact for each engaged sense. An EM-marketer may decide to involve all senses. However impact of the same programme will not be the same for all consumers. Some people are naturally more audio (hearing) oriented while others are comparatively more receptive and naturally engaged in visual communications (sight). If a communication is on radio, the salience of the experience for the audio-oriented consumer would naturally be higher than for the latter consumer, who would find relatively greater experiential salience in a billboard advertisement.

This we can express as an interaction between the:

sense being engaged × frequency of engagement × salience of the engaged sense for the consumer for given frequency

2. What is consumer's need for involvement in the experiential process given both past and current consumption situations. This is a factor of the consumer's need for relational involvement and the specific situation characteristics. There is an inherent assumption that most EM proponents have been making – that all consumers would want to relate to the brand all the time. There is little existing research evidence to accept this notion without large caveats. Some of the people you meet in life, you just want to meet them again. Some others you simply wish to avoid as much as possible. Most people you have no specific likes or dislikes at initial interaction and you just go with the flow depending on how subsequent interactions, if any, should pan out in the future. People are not equally relationally oriented to all people in their lives. As described in Chapter 3 people have different levels of relationships and some way of categorizing 'relational others' in reference to themselves.

As similarly, some consumers will want to relate to your brand, some others will not. Most, however, will wait and see what you are all about before they commit themselves to the relationship. It is important to understand that the relational orientation of the consumer will determine the consumer's experienced intensity. This relational orientation will also be factor of past experiences and consumption contexts the consumer has travelled through with the brand as well as with competing brands.

This we can express as an interaction between:

relational orientation of consumer based on past experiences × specific situational characteristics of current consumption situation

3. Mode of Cognition and Emotional Node: Each individual is experientially triggered at different points in time to respond to certain stimuli in a particular way. Some days you wake feeling peppy and fresh, wanting to party with your noisiest friends or maybe do something new and exciting. Some other days you feel quieter, more thoughtful, or just want to read a book all by yourself or listen to some soulful music. Some other days you feel creative and colourful wanting to twang on your guitar, wear that exotic perfume, or go riding off on your bike in the rain. Other times you are feeling out-of-sorts, wanting to play some mindless, thoughtless computer game which has very few 'buttons' and is rather repetitive in skill. All these choices of activities are driven by largely uncontrolled modes of thought (cognition) and nodal emotions that all normal adults experience through each day. Depending on the modes and nodes, people decide upon complimentary or supplementary activities because they seek the related experiences. As opposed to relational orientation, this is referred to as the 'experiential seek' of a consumer. Marketers have recognized the effect of these cognitive modes and emotional nodes in different ways albeit intuitively. Some call it the personality (mistakenly so as personality is far more enduring) while others refer to this as the individual's temperament or mood (mistakenly, for mood is far too transitory and is easily changed). The construct of 'experiential seek' of the consumer on the other hand is a consumption perspective which acknowledges that two people with similar 'moods' could seek different experiences. For example, a person feeling sombre may seek a supplementing experience by listening to music in a quiet sophisticated upper-end bar while another sombre-feeling person may want to 'snap-out-of-it' and thus seek a complimentary experience by walking into a noisy mall.

This 'experiential seek' we can express as an interaction between the:

cognitive Mode × emotional Node of consumer in current consumption situation

The benefit and rationale of understanding consumers in terms of their modes of thought and nodes of emotion has significant strategic implications. This is explained in detail subsequently.

4.2.2 Experiential Salience: Nature of Experience

Nature of experience refers to whether the overall association with the set of related past experiences is considered desirable or undesirable. This is distinct from consumer attitude – which is usually categorized as positive or negative. Several EM proponents have confused positive interactions (service successes) to mean desirable experiences and negative interactions (service failures) to mean the same as undesirable experiences. This is a serious bogeyman on the back of EM. Jet Airways (see box) had a significant 'service failure' where the author along with some 40 others in the busload was taken to a 'wrong flight' as hapless passengers. The attitude towards the airline efficiency took a serious dip but the experience was enjoyable! I fell in love with the airline then – *after their service failure!* Since that experience I always think of the airline not as this super efficient, hard-nosed professional but as a sincere concerned human being who also makes mistakes and owns up with red-faced embarrassment!

'Attitudes' and 'Experiences' Are Different: A Jet Airways Experience

Once I was travelling from Ahmedabad to Mumbai at the end of a very hard day at work. All checks and clearances done, I stood in queue with other passengers – most of them as tired looking as myself. We got onto the awaiting bus in silence to reach the flight we were to board. We got off the bus just as silent and disinterested in any happenings around us. It was after all just another flight and we were all insipidly tired. We alighted from the bus and lined up like silent sheep. The efficient airline employee at the foot of the ladder took one look at the first boarding pass and went red in the face. He then grinned sheepishly at us and told us that this flight was to Indore and not Mumbai !

As we clambered back onto the bus, moving to our 'right' flight to Mumbai, the dispirited and tired busload of 40 odd passengers had miraculously changed into this bunch of giggly school kids having so much fun wondering about which city we were going to be taken to by Jet now! Such exotic fantasies we shared amongst ourselves living our moment of sheer ludicrousness!

Was it a grand service failure? Yes, certainly so. Did it cause a negative dip in attitude regarding airline 'efficiency'? Yes, any attitude measure would have reflected that – especially in the 'structured' in-flight questionnaire measuring service performance and attitudes that the airline constantly circulates to its passengers. But was it a negative experience? *Certainly not!* It was an adorable experience and helped all passengers connect with each other and with the 'human face' of the airline. It lifted our tired spirits and made us all so very cheerful! Even after a year I still smile at my recollections of that day.

We all have arguments with our friends, sometimes even a good fight. But does one single argument mean all past experience of that relationship stands negated? Normal adults are not swayed by 'recency effects' in relationships to such an extent. Often arguments that are resolved satisfactorily lead to better understanding and improved relationships. As long as attitudes and experiences are confused or used interchangeably, EM practice will remain limited.

Continuous 'positive' experiences often end up feeling predictable, monotonous and boring. And boring is not a desirable experience at all! Many EM proponents suggest a way to create a memorable experience each and every time by 'delighting the consumer'. Unfortunately, there are inherent anomalies in the 'delight' route. If each time I am delighted at the store, then next time I walk in expecting a 'delight'. So to really delight me the next time the store will have to work out a 'double delight' – one to match my existing delight expectations and the second delight dosage to exceed my expectations. The delight route is thus a dangerous trap. How many ways can you think of 'delighting' a consumer – which is also not replicable by competitors?

If you are a marketer who has been wondering how to delight your customer constantly, there may be a need to rethink that strategic focus. If your closest friend was to keep working out ways to delight you each time you met, how tiresome that would get! And how predictable and hence boring! Best relationships are formed depending on how a person tunes into your needs. They are certainly not formed by the other person constantly expecting you to fit into their mode – that too a single mode of perennial 'delight'. And as they say, no relationship should take so much effort from just one party. Best relationships are those where the relational other has a fairly predictable constant core you can 'connect' to but with many changing peripherals that keep the other person seem alive and growing and always interesting to interact with.

Why can't your brand be like that interesting relational other to your consumer?

4.3 Experiential Marketing

Experiential marketing seeks to make consumer experiences richer and more involving by employing multiple faculties and senses. It involves viewing the entire consumption experience as a holistic activity and thereby designing the entire experience so that each of its elements are in tandem with the others. EM requires engaging all the five senses as much as possible whenever the consumer expresses a desire to get in touch with the brand. A rich experience would eventually motivate the consumer to actively seek interactions with the brand and form a steady and strong relationship with the brand.

Experiential Marketing recognizes that the development of brand-consumer relationships is dependent on the individual contacts or experiences that a customer has with the brand. It recognizes that by managing these experiences, the progress of the relationship can be influenced to a large extent.

4.3.1 Understanding the Experiential Mindspace

The consumer mindspace may be defined as that part of the consumer's self that consciously imbibes and evaluates experiences. As described in the previous chapter, consumer mindspace can be broadly categorized at the first level based on the consumer's value systems and operating identity – personal identity or any of the social identities that are contextually salient. An exhaustive list of values and identities is not necessary (and neither is it possible). It is sufficient for a marketer to identify the salient values of each consumer and the salient operating identity. Based on this information, multiple personality cells can be generated. These are the different cells which the brand's consumers occupy. These cells are the personality platforms from which consumers will view any brand. Thus, two people having differing values and operating identities will make different decisions in otherwise similar consumption situations. In other words, consumers belonging to different 'value X operating identity' cells will have systematic patterns of differences in what experiences they seek and how they evaluate experiences.

Furthermore, at a second level and within each cell, perceptions and evaluations of experiences will be influenced by two individual level processes – cognitive (thought mode) and affective (emotional node). Cognitive modes and emotional nodes, as described previously, also induce systematic patterns of experience assessment amongst consumers.

Together, these four dimensions constitute the mindspace of the consumer. If all possible combinations were plotted, an individual would occupy a particular cell of this 'global' mindspace. A marketer simply needs to plan and execute strategies to address each consumer cell by fulfilling the related 'experiential seek'.

4.3.2 Levels in Experiential Marketing

Developments in brand-consumer experiential interactions take place across four broad stages. These stages can be associated well with levels in Experiential Marketing.

In the first stage, the marketer is sending out signals about the offering to the consumer, largely in terms of credence-based cues which are symbolically evaluated. Traditional marketers would be apt to call this level as benefits positioning, though it is different. The effort at this stage is to convey the experiential promise of the offering and build credibility for the promises made. This experiential positioning effort uses as many of the five senses to convey the brand persona in an effort to capture either the consumer's primary cognitive mode or the key emotional node. Usually it is the emotional node that is the focus though that may not always be the most advisable route to the consumer's relational paths. For example, a car is positioned as promising the experience of a comfortable ride to the child sleeping at the rear (which is usually a jerkier seating as compared to the front). Similarly a bookstore promises its consumers serene and comfortable surroundings with ample sitting/standing space to browse through its huge assortment of books.

In the second stage of relationship development, the marketer uses the entire consumption process to build further credibility and enhance the experiential promises. This second level thus involves some form of additions to the entire experiential value proposition. This is achieved by charting out the entire experiential flow of consumption and making complimentary and supplementary additions to the core experience, thereby enriching it. The effort is usually to appeal to the consumer's cognitive modes besides the emotional nodes. If the consumption flow suggests that consumers prefer to read a chapter before buying a book, the bookstore adds seats and tables for consumers to sit comfortably and read the initial chapters of a book before making a purchase. If consumption flow suggests that two types of consumers – those who read classics and those who read romantic novels, often want expert advice based on an understanding of their needs, the bookstore then adds two employees – one who is well-versed with classics and another who is updated with all chik-lit to advise consumers on what books suit their tastes and they could consider for purchase/gifting.

The third level is where a marketer seeks to move up the relational ladder by increasingly involving the consumer in the consumption activity. At this third level of experiential marketing, the marketer actively hunts for additional areas where experience can be provided. This stage involves an enhancement of the core experience and goes much beyond enrichment of experience. The consumer likes to sip a drink when reading a book, and so the bookstore adds coffee and tea as supplementary offerings. Some consumers like to have soft music playing when they are reading, so the store provides for some headphones and choice of music which can be accessed by a consumer who needs music.

Chapter 5 deals with the above first, second and third levels of EM in greater detail.

At the final level, the marketer explodes the relationship between the brand and the consumer into other offerings. The effort is to provide not just one set of offerings but capture all needs that address the identified consumer mindspace – cognitive modes and emotional nodes. This is executed by an extension of the current experiential offerings to related fields. All possible extended interactions of the brand with the consumer are considered and then (re)designed to reinforce the same company/brand persona consistently through multiple channels and offerings. Thus a bookstore that is experientially positioned for a contemplative consumer who wants to explore new worlds in a relaxed way, may add other offerings that appeal to the 'contemplative relaxed explorer'. These new offerings may not be related to books at all. Chapter 6 deals with this fourth level of EM in greater detail.

References

1. Subhashini Kaul and Nirmesh Mehta (2009), Note on Experiential Marketing, Working Paper IIMA, MAR0408TEC

5 Consumers as Co-producers

The traditional marketing view of the customer is of one who buys, uses and/or consumes the offering, which is created by a producer firm and often marketed by another firm under its brand name. This view renders the consumer as a passive recipient of pre-designed 'consumer value/which the firm had formulated into the offering. Whatever 'value' has been incorporated in the offering is by the design and intent of the producer-marketer. The consumer can only evaluate the offering and pass his/her judgement on how preferable and worthy that offering's value is when compared to competitors'. Thus, in traditional marketing 'consumer value' is a verb – something a firm does to and with an offering. This 'value' is distinct from the consumer's decision-making process–which is examined by a marketer post introduction of the offering just as a scientist stands and curiously watches what rats do when a piece of fresh cheese is offered into the cage!

In Experiential Marketing (EM), this duality stands questioned. Is the 'offering' really different and distinct from how a consumer perceives it? Irrespective of what a manufacturer embeds in it, the perception of the consumer is not the sole determinant of the consumer value of the offering? Can the object (the offering) be so artificially separated from the subject (the consumer) and still retain its meaningfulness?

In other words, EM views consumer value not as something a firm does but as a psychological construct of the consumer. Value is generated not in the strategic boardroom or at the manufacturing floor or even at the marketers planning desk – it is created by the consumer when the consumer 'experiences' the offering. Thus an offering is a bundle of symbolic cues and potential messages regarding consumption experience. It is only in the decoding of these symbolic cues and in conversion of potential promises to an actual usage experienced-by the consumer that the concept of 'consumer value' emerges.

Though traditional marketers have time and again openly accepted the fact that the acid-test of an offering is when it 'hits the market', yet there is complete unwillingness to abandon the philosophy of *dwaita* – meaning the dualism of subject and object.

Table: 5.1

FAQ's on implications of the non-dualistic orientation of EM
1. If offering is not separate from the consumer and I have little control on the consumer, does it mean I have little control on the offering? Then what is my job as a marketer? What shall I as the marketer control and manipulate?
A. The offering is all yours to manipulate as you deem fit. The perceived 'consumer value' is a shared construction between the producer-marketer, the 'reality' (as you the marketer perceive it) and the consumer's judgment of the offering's 'reality' (as he or she perceives it). These may coincide – but in reality they do so rarely.
2. Consumer value of offerings determines various possible market segments and target consumers amount which I as a marketer choose from. If consumer value is not distinct from consumer, then is segmentation, targeting and positioning all to be abandoned? If consumer value is not distinct from consumers and I have to start with consumers, then who shall I look upon as my segment when I wish to grow? Are marketers not in a loop of whether the egg (tentative offering) or the chicken (tentative consumer segment) should come first?

A. This is an age old debate in marketing and is a ubiquitous issue during new product introductions. This strategic issue is dealt with in Chapter 8. Suffice to say for now that tentative offerings are certainly the start point of a new business. However, offerings cannot remain as the primary point of reference. Product-centric growth strategies have several limitation, the key limitation being that they lead a firm in the wrong direction so very often. Existing research indicates that of 100 new product introductions, 60 per cent fail at the initial stages. Of the remaining which are introduced, only 40 per cent are able to sustain even in the short-term. Of the fortune 500 companies listed in 1970, less than a third were still in existence by 1983! This annihilation is the price a traditional marketer will have to pay, sooner or later, for being offering-centric. Marketers, when deciding new product innovations (and not setting up a completely new venture) need to consciously move their reference points further towards their customers.

3. What shall I use consumer research for if not to find segments given my offering and its consumer value? If consumer decides on everything, then is not the marketer rendered completely impotent with just many fancy but useless tools?

A. In EM the offering is not targeted to a pre-identified segment! In fact, the objective is to help consumers self-select themselves into your brand segment. In other words, the consumer is completely empowered to segment various brand offerings and it is the consumer who chooses your brand. The marketer does not choose the consumer. The marketer only creates, communicates and delivers an offering that the marketer 'believes' in. Consumers will only respond to that belief – and so they decide whether they like, dislike or have no specific opinion about the brand persona that is reflected in the brand behaviour and inferred attitudes. This decision is arrived at based on their experiences with your brand.

4. I tweak my offering based on research inputs to increase consumer value. If consumer value is independent of offering then what am I tweaking?

A. You are tweaking the offering and rightly so. If consumer has told you that the consumer value can improve by changing the packaging, you should go ahead and change the packaging. You have every right (and control too!) to tweak and even drastically change your offering. But remember that you are not tweaking consumer value. Any changes made in the offering for what a marketer thinks is better performance, may not necessarily enhance perceived consumer value – some changes could even reduce consumer value if your research was misleadingly, i.e. functionally oriented and not experientially designed.

> 5. What shall I believe in as a brand? I am in business for profits after all, and I am willing to have my brand showcased as believing in anything my largest consumer base wants the brand to stand for.
>
> A. Grow up. Your brand is not a child, it is a mature adult. You can of course choose the brand persona of a naive and inconsistent child that only mimics (it may also work, who knows). But the fact is that your brand will be perceived by consumers as an adult, innocent as a child or as silly as a child (if being child-like is the role you seek for your brand.) Choose what role your brand will play in the competitive relational platform where consumers, competitors and all stakeholders are watching you all the time.

The reasons for not implementing but remaining with an appreciation of the intuitively appealing *adwaita* or non-dualistic orientation to consumer value as advocated in EM stems from purely operational factors. A marketer needs to separate controllable and uncontrollable factors. Thus it is easier and simpler to think of the offering as the controllable factor and the consumer as the uncontrollable given. This notion is certainly easier to understand and perpetuate but it is certainly not correct. Developing the EM orientation is difficult – not because it is complicated to understand. In fact, EM is intuitively easier to grasp and understand. But EM becomes complex in execution. In EM it is not possible to enumerate any kind of structured 4P's or 5C's or anything remotely similar to the 7S's. Traditional marketing with its overly simplistic and rather naïve 4P and other similarly easy to list structures provides an easier handle for instructors to teach and a marketer to function with a checklist of what to pay attention to. This check-list structure is probably one key reason why the 4P product-centric structure of 'things-to-do' by a marketer became so immensely popular even though several voices were constantly calling attention to the nebulous but accurate experiential whole of a consumer.

Consider the simple 4P framework for a minute. Does the consumer think product as distinct from price, distinct from promotions and distribution? If your answer is no (except when a marketing researcher should forcibly ask a consumer to think and respond only to price!), then is the attachment to traditional marketing non-consumer-centric structures not akin to searching for lost keys in a place where there is some light and so one can see better, even though the keys to the consumer-experience lock have been lost several miles away where there is much darkness. Currently EM seems complex for the road is less travelled, not because it has revolutionary premises. The premises of EM are only those that marketers have always sensed as being more appropriate, effective and reasonable.

Accepting the *adwaita* orientation of experiential marketing gives rise to several frequently asked questions regarding operational aspects. Some of these questions have been compiled (see Table: 5.1) based on my experience with practitioners and students over the past few years.

In EM consumers are treated as co-producers of the offering and co-constructors of the meaning of consumer value embedded in the offering. Understanding the role of consumers as co-constructors of meaning and as co-producers of the offering has significant implications for the following:

1. Communicating value
2. Delivering value
3. Adding value in existing offerings, and
4. New product introductions

In this chapter we examine the potential of using consumers as co-producers in communicating, delivering and adding value. New offerings are discussed in the next chapter.

5.1 Experiential Communication and Delivery of Value

In the theory of marketing mix, promotion (communication) and place (distribution) determine where/how the offering will be communicated and where/how the product will be sold. The concept of the marketing mix itself has been largely abandoned by marketers for decades now as it is purely a firm convenience when making decisions about different elements of the offering. The marketing mix is not based at all on the consumer perspective. Several researchers have tried to come up with a marketing mix from the consumer perspective. The idea in these efforts one presumes was to incorporate the consumer perspective but also provide a handle to marketers as some list of elements to juggle with. This effort gave rise to concepts such as what is now popularly referred to as the Dolan 5 C's and the 4S, 7S models, ect. But in such efforts to make things-to-do simpler with checklist for practitioners, the consumer perspective has always had to take a back seat, often getting completely lost in the process.

EM is not in a position to simplify consumer experience into component elements as yet. The understanding of experience is still far too complex for component enumeration. It may eventually happen with further research and practice. Current effort in this chapter is to understand how business practices have become increasingly complex and how competitive value addition is possible through experiential communication and delivery. This chapter outlines some of the key concepts underlying experiential communication and delivery of value and the key issues that need to be addressed. The objective is to enable practitioners to gain ideas and possibilities for experimenting in real life with complete confidence that EM can and does work.

5.1.1 Distribution Challenges in EM

The challenge is to involve the consumer in the process of delivery of the offering at the earliest. This requires industry knowledge to be supplemented by a deep understanding of experiential marketing. Unfortunately, both these skills are seldom available with one single individual and requires several people to come together and work as a team. Whenever I mention EM in the context of any offering (product or service), the usual responses are thematically experiential in nature rather than being operationally experiential. For example, think of EM applied in the context of a restaurant. The first (and often the last) thought is of a theme restaurant – a recreated Gujarati or Rajasthani village scene where, the experiential thought goes towards creating an ambience, the decor, the furniture, the music, etc. But in delivering experiential value the *mode must shift to the consumer* as a co-producer. And this line of thinking when understood and imbibed provides several startling opportunities. A restaurant in Mumbai offers a wide range of tandoori stuff. The table at which you seat yourself has a small hole in the centre with glowing charcoal in it (a mini tandoor right at your table!). Your paneer tikkas and kebabs are brought to you partly cooked and then you can cook it yourself in whatever style you want to eat it as. Another restaurant provides all the Chinese ingredients in a large booth. You walk in there and pick up whatever you want (I once filled half my bowl with just spring onions!) and add sauces as you please (I found the one with 'apple sauce' to be most delicious) and through a glass counter you acknowledge the smiling chef, see your food getting cooked in front of you, and eat your own perfect invention! Sometimes the outcome is horrendous but I enjoy even my most atrocious concoctions. Other consumers who don't want to experiment with their food simply ask the staff person standing right there to fill their bowl for them as they stand and watch with complete curious involvement.

The beauty in the two examples given above is not in their offering 'USP' per se but in how they deliver experientially. And in this process they create a completely new experiential offering. When consumers eat at the table and say 'Hmm, this is delicious', they are including themselves in the creation of the food. The experiential involvement by including consumers in the offering creation and delivery process ensures a relational embeddedness. In how many ways, and in what stages can you involve your consumer in your offering such that the final offering has inherently greater consumer participation and involvement?

5.1.2 Complexities of Multichannel Marketing

Existing research confirms that 65-70 per cent of individuals are multichannel consumers. They use more than one channel to reach out to a brand whether to gather information, to communicate their queries or to buy. Multichannel consumers also spend significantly more than the minority group of single channel shoppers. This factor has exploded the complexity of managing channels of communication and delivery. Information availability has exploded. There are over a 100 television channels and scores of radio channels available in multiple languages to consumers in general. Those with access to the net whether through the internet cafes, home computers or their blackberrys and mobiles have even greater choice of channels to access information. Each channel has an inherently different experiential seek. Accessing the net in different places (cafe, home, workplace) all have different consumption experiences for a consumer.

Despite this proliferation, multichannel marketing is still in its infancy and research knowledge in this field is rather limited. Companies are still struggling to understand various new channels such as the net and the mobile and several misguided attempts to treat them in the traditional marketing-mix way have failed. In such a situation it is impossible for companies to take a holistic view of how their channels compliment and supplement each other. Most companies take a 'tactical approach' and view each channel in isolation simply because doing otherwise makes the task impossible to manage. Unfortunately this approach of ticking off from a list of things-to-do, does not even consider consumer value forget about consumer experience. It is assumed that each channel represents a particular segment of consumers with somewhat distinct communication and delivery of value needs. But with multiple channel access and information explosion this difference is no longer tenable unless one takes a magnifying glass to chart channel differential benefits and consumer behaviour.

Information technology is a fantastic enabler, the true potential of which is far from being achieved. Here is one example of how IT can help a consumer be involved in a product delivery as narrated to me by a friend of mine. A brand of hair-oil conducted research and found that people have not just three types of hair (oily, normal and dry) but very many hair types. The hair-oil consumer also has many kinds of hair problems which could be temporary, seasonal and contextual (for example I need to grow my hair long in next three months before my engagement function). Research told the company that about 10 odd-basic hair-oil ingredients when mixed a particular way take care of most hair types and hair problems. The delivery system then became simple and experiential. The consumer was co-opted to become a co-producer of hair-oil. An interactive kiosk would ask a few questions which the consumer answered on current condition of their own hair, shoved in an empty bottle from the nozzle and out would pour the 'right' kind of hair-oil at one month of usage!

Customized paneer tikkas and chinese food is not less or more easier to achieve than customized hair-oil. Calling upon the consumer as a co-producer achieves one-on-one offerings, and perfect customization. In this the consumer is never required to 'learn or educate' himself beyond what knowledge he/she already possesses about the self and his own needs. It is precisely in this light that one states that the application of EM simply to one-on-one interactive communication is far too limiting of the actual potential of EM.

5.1.3 Communication Challenges in EM

Research indicates that some consumers prefer to collect all relevant information and muse about decision-making while other consumers prefer to collect information in bits and pieces, process it and then decide what further data they need. Today's consumer actively seeks information, when needed. The explosion in channels (of information and delivery) means that these active consumers no longer will attune themselves to what and how a marketer chooses to furnish as information. Consumer's right to accurate and complete information is also being increasingly acknowledged in Indian laws. Even while searching for such information, consumers want to have a pleasant experience and they will move to the competitor who caters better to their information needs in an experiential way. A channel that does not provide that information or the product itself is quickly abandoned because there are so many alternatives available.

As early as the 60's-70's, Herbert Simon predicted that '...in an information-rich world, the wealth of information means a dearth of something else: a scarcity of whatever it is that information consumes. What information consumes is rather obvious: it consumes the attention of its recipients (p40-41). The effect of the channel and channel information explosion has certainly and drastically reduced consumer attention span. TV ads Aired every 15 minutes are often muted or through technology even paused/fast forwarded. The basic premise of mass advertising is based on attention which then leads to recall. Without attention, recall is naturally non-existent. Marketers have tried all gimmicks – including humour, controversy and sex in images. Consumers notice the ads, even remember them but they do not associate it with any brand in particular. By the time the brand name flashes in the ad consumer's attention span is over. Research indicates that sexual images in advertisements have stopped grabbing extra attention span compared to other ads for a while now.

Relevancy and privacy in information are key issues for communicating with consumers given the limited attention they wish to devote to brands. This relevant and private information has to be made available at convenient timings as selected by consumers. Any channel they access needs to provide the relevant information while maintaining their privacy. In some ways, the consumer wants everything for nothing right up to the actual exchange. The consumer today demands free and accurate information as and when it is desired and in the form it is desired. Thus communication methods need to become increasingly personalized.

This is an enormous communication challenge where the IT department of an organization needs to be head-on into managing. EM requires IT systems as a significant enabler. Unfortunately, in most organizations 'communications strategy' is a marketing manager's problem and not the IT manager's job. And understanding technical aspects of IT is not required of a marketing manager. With such silos of organizational functioning, everything about consumer experience rests only between the stools.

EM sets a challenge for IT within an organization to manage net and website content in such a way that a consumer can easily zoom into the appropriate information that she seeks and filter out irrelevant information. The challenge is not to provide copious information as the firm thinks is relevant, but the focus in EM is to address consumer attention scarcity by providing easy and timely access to what the consumer thinks is relevant. The idea should be to enhance information search and communication experience.

Communication using these modern methods can easily become two way. Two-way communications help immensely in enhancing the experiential salience and thus in building strong relationships. EM has to be facilitated by available advances in information technology that allow the organizations to maintain and analyse the history of relationships with each and every customer using customer relationship management (CRM) software. Maintaining a database of personal information allows a phenomenal scope for customization and personalized attention. Each organization has this tool available at its disposal. How it can be used is only limited by the cognitive and creative abilities of each organization. Such customization is beneficial to the seller because it engenders loyalty. Regular customers are less expensive to cater to. They also provide free word-of-mouth promotions and referrals which in today's marketplace has greater credibility and network reach effects than traditional company sponsored communications. For the consumer, the advantage lies in feeling specially catered to in a mutually-fulfilling relationship.

5.2 Experiential Additions to Consumer Value

Generic value addition happens when a manufacturer vertically integrates to increase value addition by the firm. For example, a small dairy farm were to start processing its own milk into milk related by-products. This increases the value of firm operations but as far as the consumer is concerned there is no experiential value-addition. Experiential additions to consumer value occur when a firm identifies and addresses a new need in the entire consumption space with a modified offering. In this section I refer to ways and means by which such experiential value adds for the consumer can be undertaken and managed.

5.2.1 Anchored Experiential Value-Additions

As long as differentiation and value-addition are based on unanchored dimensions, replication will continuously happen. In such replication, competitors, as the shade meters example shows (see Table: 5.2), are not restricted to the product category but encompasses all those who can and will use the 'symbol' with a similar meaning. Too many brands attaching themselves to a particular symbol will only dilute the symbol. This dilution will be experienced even by the first-mover. With so many shade meters, the consumer is no longer sure the meter indicates any unique credibility claim in any product category anymore. No brand will gain anymore from this 'shade-meter-assurance' value addition. It is no longer a meaningful value addition even for the brand that inaugurated this value addition. Yet, not giving out a shade meter will mean a brand will lose out to competition, and so net effect is that not giving a shade meter can be a value deletion in some cases. In a few months time, the shade meter has become a product necessity for any offering entailing a shade difference.

Table: 5.2

Unanchored value additions : The shade meter replication

Consider the whiteness shade meter. One is no longer sure who started with this idea first but it is currently all over the place. When the idea first came about, measurement indicated some sort of service guarantee to the consumer. After all, why would a detergent powder give a shade meter if it was not certain that consumer shade meter usage would show a significant difference. But now not just detergents but a host of unrelated products attach a shade meter as a default product accessory. Beauty creams and fairness creams give a shade meter (of various shades of wheatish-colour for the Indian skin) so you can check your complexion shade before and after two/three weeks of use. There is also a white shade meter which assures you that the rest of the body will become as fair as your face. There is also a toothpaste available with a shade meter so you can measure the increased whiteness of your teeth.

Perhaps drycleaners should also start handing out shade meters soon – so the consumer can check the shade before and after a cleaning to reassure themselves that the shade of clothes has not changed!

Not just experientially but relationally too, the shade meter is a cross-eyed cue. Why should the brand presume that the loyal consumer is a suspicious other who will not believe the claims of the brand? Is a detergent not supposed to clean? If a detergent tells a loyal consumer that white clothes will become whiter, why should that consumer not believe the claim? Was the detergent actually talking to competitors by throwing this shade meter challenge? If the consumer perceives no marked difference in your claim as compared to competitors, then the shade meter is not going to help anyways. If on the other hand overall credibility of the entire product category is a problem (e.g. lets say most consumers believe fairness creams always perform below their expectations), then is the shade meter really an assurance?

Relationships, as described in Chapter 3 are not a factor of who moved in first. They are a factor of who moves in closest to the customers. Consider advertisements that in the recent past associated themselves with patriotism symbols. From clothes to cars to soaps and detergents, everything became a matter of national pride! Consumers probably did not register any of those brands as being nationalistic. The Raymond's emotion displayed by its Complete man were replicated by so many other brand advertisements. Raymond stayed on the course undaunted by competing claims to its experiential platform. It only did more of what it believed the brand stood for. Today, take any ad of any other product that takes an emotional appeal similar to Raymond; chances are that the consumer is still thinking about Raymond when watching the ad.

5.2.2 Anchor with Your Audience: Who Are You Communicating with?

Value additions need to be planned experientially and relationally. If a value addition is designed to attract strangers to your camp, then check if your 'friends' are going to find your value addition acceptable, confusing or deplorable. I have listed below some of the most common and recurring aspects of EM failure.

Confusing 'brand friends' with a generic communication

The shade meter is an example of a detergent brand talking to 'strangers' and 'acquaintances' and perhaps even competitors while several 'friends' are present in the gathering as well. If a friend of yours should suddenly say, 'You know I never lie to you', then you are probably left wondering what he lied about recently!

Mistaking 'friends' for 'acquaintances'

A particular branded apparel store in Ahmedabad was my most favourite store. I spent several thousands of rupees there each year for as many as seven years. I seldom visited any other store. I was a brand ambassador of sorts for that store, dragging family and friends, who saw me transformed into this 'let's not waste time at other stores' kind of a person when it came to apparel shopping. That year the store (as usual) invited me to their special sale. Unlike previous years, this time I was not travelling and so I visited the store. The store's 'fashion consultant' who I always preferred to interact with each time I shopped there told me that loyal customers were informed specially of the sale a day before so we could browse around peacefully and get our pick. All other hoi polloi would walk in the next day.

My grin aimed at him was meant to say 'Oh! you made special happy hours for me as I am your friend! Thanks!'

But with ample time and special freedom to browse I noticed that my last month's rather heavy purchases (including that beautiful multi-coloured full sleeved shirt that I so loved and thought them to be exquisitely expensive) were all marked down by 50-60 per cent!

I was aghast! Why didn't you tell me, your *'friend'*, to defer my purchases by a month especially if you had so much stock left? My question left the 'fashion consultant' aghast.

I have never visited that brand's store in any of the cities ever again. I now visit any and all other apparel stores. I have become a 'promiscuous apparel shopper' because of a relational betrayal.

My relational orientation to apparel stores is not so trusting anymore. Is there any store out there that can reach out to me, help me overcome my existing hurt of betrayal by this branded-apparel store and be my true friend?

5.2.3 Missing out on Post-Purchase as Part of Consumption Experience

A good competitor is all that is required to dislodge a brand that has ignored post-purchase and post-consumption experiences for too long. There is a well-reputed national brand of jams that I have enjoyed since childhood. But I could never, ever, open the bottle myself. For several years I have had someone else open it for me but recently I find this 'uncaring' attitude of the brand getting on my nerves. There is probably some sort of vacuum sealing that makes it impossible for a feeble hand as mine to open it. I always have to cut open the lid. This meant that for years I had to stock the opened jam bottle in the fridge, this would eventually dry up the top layers and the bottle has to be thrown away immediately after use (because the bottle is lidless and not reusable). I always felt I was paying extra for the glass bottle which was supposed to be used and reused but the company made sure I couldn't! Now I have shifted to another brand of jams, the taste is different (but nice) but most importantly the bottle is so easy to open. I can also reuse the bottle post consumption for storing other things.

Too often marketers forget that post-purchase usage and disposal of the offering also constitutes a critical part of the consumption experience. While disposal is considered by marketers for offerings that are hazardous or unhygienic (e.g. medical waste), daily products also afford significant scope for value addition during disposing.

5.2.4 Using Overt Actions to Convey Abstract Concepts

With an experiential consumer you will frequently come across abstract words such as 'restless', 'helpless', 'lost', 'uncomfortable', 'unsure', 'confused', etc. These consumer states are transitory cognitive modes and/or emotional nodes when into a consumption situation that does not necessarily need overt addressing. Covert symbols often convey the needed message. Marketers often tend to address abstract consumer needs through overt and hard-hitting messages that are more damaging than helpful. Confronting consumer fears and confusions head on is not a bright thing to do. The earlier health awareness campaigns which had a stark fear appeal caused consumers to get up and switch their TV off especially when they were aired around dinner time. It is a natural human tendency to block unsavory messages that tell them that they are inadequate and fearful/negligent/confused as individuals. Consumers are not fools and if you think they are fools who need a message to be hammered into their heads, they will often respond by ignoring you. For years voting was conveyed as a duty of a citizen. The message was clear, overt, unambiguous and hard-hitting. You fail as a citizen if you don't vote. Consumers ignored it. The 'pappu can't vote' campaign was a far subtler message which was not overtly preachy and so lowered consumer resistance to listening. The successful message was conveyed symbolically rather than overtly.

5.2.5 Anchoring with too Generic or too Specific Symbols

A brand of paint tells me that whenever I see colour, I should think of them. It is not possible. Consequently, I never think of them at all. The symbolism association is too generic though highly relevant to the offering only if it is seen from a marketer's perspective. But symbols must have meaning for consumers, not to marketers who are in love with their offering. Similarly, for a specific company logo that means nothing otherwise or is too specific, a lot of brand effort needs to go in before it can be associated with desired meaning. I have seen many firms overreach themselves believing that they can chart out a new course and educate the consumer about the brand experience.

It is sometimes necessary to do so. But it makes far greater sense to use, as far as possible, existing symbolic associations that are culturally relevant and have years of consumer learning behind them. Why spend money and effort in asking a consumer to develop associations of tradition with an apple tree when using a banyan tree would convey your brand philosophy well enough?

References

1. Guinness, Os (1994). The Dust of Death: The Sixties Counterculture and How It Changed America Forever, Second edition, Crossway Books
2. Judd and Alexander (1983), On the reduced effectiveness of some sexually suggestive ads, Journal of the *Academy of Marketing Science*, 11 (1-2)
3. Simon, H. A. (1971), "Designing Organizations for an Information -Rich World", in Martin Greenberger, *Computers, Communication, and the Public Interest*, The Johns Hopkins Press, ISBN 0-8018-1135-X
4. Simon, H. A. (1996), *The Sciences of the Artificial* (3rd ed.), The MIT Press, ISBN 0-262-69191-4.
5. Vandermerwe, Sandra (2000), How Increasing Value to Customers Improves Business Results, *Sloan Management Review*, 42 (1)

6 Experiential New Offerings

The EM route to growth and planning of new offerings is certainly not the only route. I list below two other commonly used methods to select new offerings and plan an organizations growth strategy. Each route has its advantages and disadvantages and a comparison will help understand the EM ments and benefits of the route to growth.

6.1 Route One: Competency-Centric Growth

In this route the new offerings capitalize on the existing competencies and competitive advantages of the firm. A toothpaste manufacturer who perceives his distribution network as being far more efficient as compared to competition, will search for opportunities and expand into those opportune offerings that can be delivered through the same channel. The offerings are not necessarily in the same product category, the only tenon for selection of new offerings is the delivery-competency overlap.

6.2 Route Two: Profitability-Centric Growth

Several organizations look for profitable ventures that can add a cool 30 per cent to the bottom line. The new offerings are determined and decided upon based on profitability potential. Each offering and its markets are examined as a new venture drawing little or nothing from existing ventures. Such organizations are often into a wide variety of offerings, assimilated over a period of time. The same group of companies then includes within its fold tyres, retail, pharmaceuticals, chemicals and mobile services. Such organizations create distinct brands in each market they are addressing. Sometimes the group brand name is just an assurance of basic trust and quality having no other symbolic associations because the individual brands in such a disparate market have distinative positioning statements and this a unique brand persona of their own.

6.3 Route Three: EM-Centric Growth

EM principles recommend a firm stay with the selected target consumer with the identified experiential seek. As mentioned in Chapter 4, let us say a bookstore started by addressing the 'contemplative relaxed explorer' who operates primarily from the personal identity with a key value of 'being considered as an intellectual'. The bookstore will need to explore growth opportunities not based on the offering of books but based on the experiential promises made to this segment of consumers. In other words, a natural extension in business for this bookstore is not a magazines store or a music store or even a second hand bookstore. A natural extension is one that instantly appeals to the experiential seek of the 'contemplative relaxed explorer operating from the personal identity of an intellectual'. What offerings would appeal to this experiential seek?

As mentioned briefly in Chapter 4, EM suggests that new offerings should be consumer-centric rather than firm-centric. In other words, a firm does not plan a new offering because it is building on its core competency of excellent distribution network, or because it had worked out a higher inventory turnover, or because it can manufacture at lower prices. All these are firm-centric advantages. These are not consumer-centric at all. The Virgin group has amply proven that core competency anchored in an offering is a mere figment of a firm's imagination. This incorporates music records, airlines, mobiles and financial services. How much of 'core competency' can one see in that?

While most practitioners are able to appreciate all principles of EM mentioned so far, they have a rather hard time accepting the EM route to growth and new offerings. Core competency is what the CEO has built over a number of years and EM is asking him/her to abandon that attachment? This is shocking in its extreme. To think of a bookstore expanding into the business of offering holiday packages to the 'contemplative relaxed explorer' seems too surreal and ludicrous. Even the example of the Virgin group is seen as an exception rather than an application of EM growth principles. For this reason, I pen down several arguments that I usually make to the disbelievers most of whom are involved in marketing strategy and related decision-making positions in large organizations. These are questions that the reader needs to answer for his/her own organization in preparation for developing an EM-orientation.

6.3.1 What Have you Developed Within Your Organization?

If your answer is a firm-specific capability which is also perhaps linked with your existing set of offerings, then much as I respect your effort, I will question your objective. If your answer is anything other than what your organization has achieved with its consumers, my questions will stay. If you accepted the initial premise that a brand is worth only as much as it has created in terms of brand-consumer relationships, then what you have achieved must be assessable in brand-consumer relational terms.

6.3.2 Who is Your Consumer?

If your consumer is described in offering centric terms, then the questions of whether you are indeed offering a branded product/service or a branded 'experience' will naturally be asked. And if you do define your consumer in experiential terms (using identity descriptions, cognitive modes and emotional nodes) then where is the question of being attached to the offering? Should not your attachment be with the experiential seek of your target consumer?

6.3.3 Who are Your Competitors?

If you define your competitors in offering-centric terms (all toothpaste marketers are competing with my toothpaste), then are you product oriented or experience oriented? EM principles do not suggest that you forget offering-centric competition. EM only suggests that you move away from mere offering-centric definitions of your market and competition and pursue the consumer relationally using the experiential orientation. Anyone talking to the 'contemplative relaxed explorer' is competition for our bookstore which is 'targeting' the same consumer. It could be a travel agency providing short holiday packages to that consumer. The key to understanding the EM route to growth is to appreciate how relationships build and sustain. If you are a contemplative brand who offers good advice, a relaxed time and interesting conversation then each time a consumer wants that experiential seek, he/she will want (*should* want) to come to you. If you have offerings to cater to that need across board and across all consumption situations of that experiential seek, it will be great. Else it is simply a lost opportunity. Also, another brand in a different product or service category, which provides a similar experiential seek, will erode your claims to that experiential positioning.

If Virgin were to offer a cola drink, what do you think will be the positioning? Does Virgin need to make any significant effort to convey a positioning for its cola drink? And how strong will that '*think hatke*' cola drink positioning be as compared to competing cola drinks that are only into that particular offering category? In fact if Virgin were to move into any market, any offering, competitors who are targeting the smart, energetic, rebellious and youthful consumer will have a hard run to convince their consumers about their existing positioning being more intense than that of Virgin's.

With each new extension into the same consumer mindspace, less and less effort will be required because the consumer already knows what the brand is all about. New offering introductions will need practically no effort over time. The brand (with its myriad offerings) then surrounds the consumer in all consumption contexts and is like a known friend with an understood brand personality who is available whenever the consumer wishes to interact with it. To achieve this, the brand presence must cut across marketer defined product and service categories. The brand presence therefore must be dictated only by the experiential seek of its target consumer.

For example, Tata is a brand name that I associate with reliability, honesty and responsible caring. In other words I have a distinct cognitive mode association with the brand though an emotional node is missing. Whenever I as a consumer (depending on my cognitive mode and emotional node) want to interact with such a brand persona, the Tata brand would gain immensely by simply being around. I as the consumer with that specific cognitive experiential seek as a need, would then make the effort to seeks the specific offering in whatever product/ service category I need at that time. How can this extend to the consumption process with the existing Tata offerings? Let us say I buy a Tata car. The car is experientially all about responsible driving, caring and reliability. What else will I as a consumer seek in that cognitive mode when driving the Tata car? Let us take my concern when on the Mumbai-Pune expressway where I drive often thinking what will happen in case there is an accident? Can the Tata car services include a distress number for emergency services (after all if the Tata brand is promising to help me in time of accidents, I will certainly believe them given the brand personification as it stands for me, right?). Several car brands that stand for reliability have done so already. Why not extend your offerings into every sphere where I as a consumer need a specific experiential seek – from salt to steel. Similarly why should the brand not be available when I look for reliability and honesty when buying mutual funds, or when I am looking for someone to help me set up IT systems at my workplace; and if you believe this is already true of the Tata brand then imagine how much intense would be the brand persona if it added an emotional node as well.

A brand cannot be everything to everybody. This is a well accepted fact though it has always been perceived as making consumer offerings centric. This statement has in the past been interpreted to mean that all segments of the market of an offering cannot be satisfied by one single brand. However, in EM this statement is offering free. An experiential brand can satisfy only a specific experiential seek. And this experiential seek is irrespective of offering limitations.

> A brand that stands for a consistent personality and an experiential seek across different product and service categories will naturally have a stronger and more intense brand persona as compared to competitors operating in a single sphere of the market with just one offering.

7 Experiential Organizations

An experiential organization (EO) is centred around consumer experiences. In providing consumer experiences, all functions, activities and departments of the organization are co-ordinated in an interdependent manner. Strategy, marketing, finance, operations, systems and manufacturing are all united seamlessly in delivering the branded unique experiential consumer value proposition.

7.1 Characteristics of Experiential Employees

Experiential employees (EE) are proud to have the social identity of being part of the organization. In all my experience as a corporate employee taking an insider view and then as researcher with an outsider perspective, I have always found people overtly comfortable as individuals in workplaces where they are proud to be working. In organizations with poor social identity constructions I have invariably met transactional employees who are simply looking at the price (salary and perk) tags – something consumers do when brands make little sense to them! There is a fair amount of research (though nascent) into what constitutes an EE, however how one can develop an EE becomes an organizational orientation and has to be driven right from the top. An EE is happy to meet the consumer, even if it is not his or her job role to meet consumers. The EE wants to know how his/her contribution helps the consumer's experiential seek. The EE is proud to know that consumers have such a wonderful relationship with a brand that he/she is part of as an employee. The EE feels ownership of the brand because he/she has helped co-construct the brand meaning for the consumer.

Research indicates that front-line people who inherently believe that their job is to help the consumer perform much better than those who do not see their roles as having such personal meaning. Organizations have addressed this need for involved employers in two ways: a) by hiring people who have such 'helpful' attitudes, and/or b) providing skill-training to people so they can 'behaviourally' demonstrate the desired helpful behaviours. Both of these approaches are misinformed and hence hardly what I call a solution. As Freidman (Rabbi, Bethesda Jewish Congregation) aptly puts it, 'The colossal misunderstanding of our time is the assumption that insight will work with people who are unmotivated to change'. When people are motivated to change, they make the effort to seek out skills and equip themselves to do their jobs better. Providing skills does not change ones attitude or substitute for the inherent lack of motivation. One large Indian retailer found that their retail store personnel were uncomfortable in dealing with the upper class, SEC A, English-speaking shoppers who visited their stores. The store personnel were often feeling disoriented in the store which was so different from their modest homes and poor living conditions. This discomfort often manifested itself as unhelpful or even rude behaviour towards shoppers. The company decided to launch a special five-day programme for the staff members which had the sole purpose of improving the self-esteem of the participants. No skill inputs on 'how to behave helpfully' were provided in those five days. No inputs were given about what 'our consumers expect as service quality'. No lectures were administered about 'our organizational philosophy of service'. The programme was simply focused on the participants to make them think of themselves as having the complete ability to move from '*zero se hero*'. Staff returned from this unique experiential programme with new found confidence, no longer uncomfortable about their social class being so different from the social class of the shoppers. All by themselves they interpreted their front-line jobs as being of help to the shoppers who were looking lost within the store. With this new sensitivity in place, each staff personnel made an extra effort to learn whatever 'skills' that were needed to help shoppers efficiently! Unfortunately, this uniquely experiential route to the employee and to consumer-service quality was a little time-consuming and too complexly abstract for business managers to understand or appreciate.

7.2 Characteristics of an Experiential Organization (EO)

An experiential organization (EO) understands that investments in employers will seldom provide results in the short-term. In an EO, a training initiative as mentioned above would have been understood across board as an activity which will only show results once an initial number of personnel have been covered by the programme.

An experiential organization (EO) is one that addresses relational and identity needs of its employees, recognizing that employees also have a particular experiential seek when they are in a place day-after-day for months and years. However, too often people mistake an EO to be an 'emotionally charged, innovative organization' with 'laughter and fun'. This is as miserably inadequate an assessment of an EO as associating experiential restaurants with theme villages! Employees are different as individuals, they have different experiential seeks. Extroverts may feel great with lots of after-office and during-office gatherings, introverts will be most unhappy. A largely feeling-based person may feel an intense sense of belonging in an emotionally charged workplace, but a thought-based person will feel scared or disenchanted. Differences in employees need to be recognized and accommodated. Some key aspects that can act as guidelines for developing the experiential orientation within an organization are given below:

1. Employer brand: The EO is characterized by a consistent and all-encompassing belief that the company is a living entity with its own unique personality and value systems. All employees are aware and share those 'core' values consciously and because those 'core' values give meaning to their own lives. In other words, an EO is foremost an employer brand in its own right.
2. Pervasive knowledge of the relational consumer: All employees in an EO whether directly in contact with the consumer or otherwise, are aware of the experiential consumer. Each function and department understands 'how' what they do at work makes a difference directly or indirectly to the experiential consumer and the brand-consumer relationship.
3. Financial gain is not primary: The effort in EO's is to stand up for what the company is all about as a personified brand. The collective brand (comprising the employees) seek to evolve as any other human being does – keeping core values constant and adapting to external environment as needed.

In other words, an EO has a strategic vision of 'who the company wants to be like as it grows up' and its mission statements are about 'what all things it would like to experiment with and dabble in' to grow up to become that envisioned, well-adjusted adult. The vision statement should be a representation of the core and desirable values. The mission statements are about what peripherals the company will use to achieve that vision. Over the lifetime of a company (assuming perpetuity) mission statements could undergo several revisions. The vision would seldom change if drafted with relational care and experiential deliberation.

A vision statement that does not incorporate anything specific is bound to lead to an organization that will flounder in bad times. For example, the different vision statements given in Table: 7.1 are sound business visions, but they have no experiential anchors and provide no clue of what kind of a 'person' the company brand would grow up to be. Employees will not be able to identify with a pure business vision of profitability and growth. People only identify and connect with people and personifications. Companies incorporate 'values' in their vision and mission statements with little understanding that these values are the core of an employer brand and sooner or later must be experientially communicated and delivered to the employees consistently. As far as employees are concerned, they need to be treated as consumers of the company brand offering. All EM principles then apply to the company brand and also engendering loyalty amongst employees just as EM principles help develop loyalty amongst consumers.

Table: 7.1

Experientially unanchored vision statements: Some examples

'---- group shall deliver everything, everywhere, everytime for every Indian consumer in the most profitable manner.'

'To be a world class organization having global network, focusing on environment friendly engineering of plastic products, providing a wide range of services and tapping other opportunities in niche markets.'

'We want to be a global leader delivering enterprise business management products and solutions.'

An experientially anchored statement of purpose: An example

'--- our purpose' is to improve the quality of life of the communities we serve.

We do this through leadership in sectors of economic significance, to which the group brings a unique set of capabilities. This requires us to grow aggressively in focused areas of business.

Our heritage of returning to society what we earn evokes trust among consumers, employees, shareholders and the community. This heritage is being continuously enriched by the formalization of the high standards of behaviour expected from our employees and companies.

'--- (our) name is a unique asset representing leadership with trust. Leveraging this asset to enhance group synergy and becoming globally competitive is our chosen route to sustained growth and long-term success'.

4. Sharing of knowledge: An EO is characterized by constant updation and sharing of thoughts, opinions and knowledge. All employees are a part of small collectives/ a team that would make time to meet and share such knowledge.

One of the key limitations of marketing, especially in practicing EM is sharing of such knowledge. The strategic oversight of a select few at the head office seldom percolates down the line even to those who are in direct contact with consumers. Strategy limits itself to branding related legislation while operation managers are considered a separate executive body. The CEO acts as the judiciary that steps in whenever the legislative and executive powers are in conflict.

There are far too many prescriptive organizations that believe that 'it is waste of time and effort to explain the strategy to employees who won't understand'. That may be true to a certain extent, but all employees are intuitively capable of understanding the experiential consumer that the organization is co-constructing meaning with. This need not necessarily mean presentations and meetings and overt efforts. Kaya skin clinic has undertaken one symbolic effort to convey the instore experience to employees who are not in direct touch with the consumer by creating a façade of the store within the head-office premises. The façade is a small but constant reminder to non-frontline personnel of what brand persona they are helping-create through their back-end and support functions.

7.3 How to Create an Experiential Organization

One useful way to create an experiential organization is to recruit and develop consumer-centric managers in strategic/ key positions. This is relatively easier than chasing the utopia of hiring a whole group of experientially oriented employees. Once key people in the organization understand company persona and the principles of experiential marketing, they naturally spread it across to other employees. However, experiential orientation is more an attitude rather than a skill or a factor of number of years of work experience, and hence is not always readily assessable by an interviewee who is himself/herself not familiar with that orientation.

Experiential organizations (EOs) would tend to use technology as an enabler. To help co-construct customized meanings with each and very one of your consumers, technology is a necessity. But technology is always just an enabler. It cannot replace the human touch. Consumers develop relationships with people, not with technology. In my personal experience, EOs tend to describe what they are doing in terms of what is achieved (or sought to be achieved) from consumer experience rather than technical specification of processes.

EOs tend to be somewhat loyal to their employees. If values and relational orientations match, then employees are special 'relationships' for the organization. Other issues are considered as just a matter of adjustment that happens in all relationships. EOs also have higher investments in employee development. Experiential managers often help their staff members learn not just what is necessary to do their existing jobs better, but invest in them to grow upwards and laterally too. Sometimes such investments are not even directly related to the job at all. Relationships grow and enhance when both parties are growing and sharing. Making training investments in one's employees helps them grow and keeps them feeling experientially alive and connected to the organization. Of course, the EO is an organization that is itself growing, staying abreast of the latest techniques and technology and always retaining that critical unique employer brand.

EOs also tend to have stronger social relationships and identities within the organization. Often this can be achieved by using smaller cross-functional teams in balanced competitive situations. These teams help generate participation and involvement while also help in sharing of information by connecting front-end employees with their support staff. The process used is by simply following an orientation that focuses on employee experience at work much in the same way that a CEO thinks consumer experience in the market!

All EO's spend time and effort on designing their organizational philosophy and in enumerating the related values. Most of these organizations seek help from time to time, whenever needed to formulate and even revisit their mission statements. Often the existing vision statement is no vision at all but a short-term marketing plan. Another problem is that too often the vision and mission clarity stays with the (new) CEO and never moves beyond to other key personnel. One way to increase the sense of common purpose is to involve as many key employees as you can when formulating the organizational philosophy and deciding what kind of a person the company should grow up to become. The vision statement (see Table: 7.1...on Tata group statement of purpose) should be achievable as a milestone but never become redundant to have experiential meaning.

Having stated my observed characteristics of EOs I must also mention that EOs are fairly ruthless when dealing with road blocks on the path to constant change and innovation. Employers who may have been with the organization since its inception are also evaluated on their ability to grow and help the company grow. Else they are replaced sooner or later.

7.4 Who Should Create an Experiential Organization?

As stated in the introduction of this book itself, EM is not a revolutionary new panacea that provides a solution for everything. Neither is EM a ubiquitous orientation that all organizations must adopt. Some organizations may want to wait a while before adopting the EM philosophy:

1. Organizations that are actors in a largely commodity market. Such organizations will gain much by simply branding their offering and creating awareness about the brand. The initial steps of branding need to be covered first. EM tools (of engaging as many senses of consumer as possible) can however be used to create such awareness and brand recall.
2. Organizations in the process of adjusting their basic marketing-mix elements. If the product or its packaging is not up to the mark as yet, experiential ways of marketing cannot cover this flaw. An organization needs to then spend time to improve the quality of its offering. The most basic premise of EM is a sound and competent offering with no existing functional quality issues.
3. Organizations that are oriented to pure profits. Several entrepreneurs ask me if EM can help them as an organizational level philosophy? Or if EM is the only sensible philosophy that is sustainable? The answer is

emphatically **'NO'**. *EM is very capable of being executed at actionable levels without bringing it to the organizational philosophy level.* Organizations that are oriented primarily (or even solely) to the bottom line are advised not to experiment with infusing the EM philosophy in their organization. Such organizations are probably into aggressive hard selling to leap into the next leagues. Small organizations that are moving into medium-scale or medium-sized organizations moving into large-scale operations need to defer EM as an organizational philosophy. EM can of course be used for communicating and delivering value, but propagating EM amongst your employees in a high-growth situation will only confuse the employees and mar your focus acment organization.

EM adoption will play rich dividends to the following kind of relatively stable organizations:

1. Those organizations that have competent, reliable offerings and are operating in a highly competitive environment. Such organizations may be small, medium or large in their turnover. EM does not necessarily need a large budget – it only needs an analytical mind, and a large 'heart'!
2. Organizations that are operating in niche markets and want to continuously build stronger brand-consumer relationships. EM can help sustain and develop these precious relationships.
3. Organizations that have clear growth objectives (group companies) and large organizations. Such organizations invariably need to create and sustain a good employer brand and practicing EM helps at both ends – with consumers as well as employees.
4. Organizations that are already into or are intending to execute philanthropic activities or discharge their

corporate social responsibilities. Often organizations select a 'cause' just because selecting and executing the organizational CSR initiatives in experientially meaningful ways will increase the relational connect with your consumers and/or employees. EM would help the organization identify causes which the consumer/employee would be experientially desirous to associate with through the brand-consumer/brand-employee relationship.

References

1. Edvardsson, B. and Mattsson, J. (1993) 'An Experienced-based Measure of Service Quality', *Service Industries Journal*, 13(4), 289-306.
2. Mick, D.G. and Buhl, C. (1992) 'A Meaning-based Model of Advertising Experiences', *Journal of Consumer Research*, 19(3), 317-338
3. Shostack, G.L. (1977) 'Breaking Free From Product Marketing', *Journal of Marketing*, 41(2), 73-80
4. Takeuchi, H. and Quelch, J. (1983), 'Quality is More Than Making a Good Product', *Harvard Business Review*, 83 (Jul/Aug), 139-145.
5. Thompson, C. (1996) 'Caring Consumers: Gendered Consumption Meanings and the Juggling Lifestyle', *Journal of Consumer Research*, 22(4), 388-408.
6. Thompson, C. (1997) 'Interpreting Consumers: A Hermeneutical Framework for Deriving Marketing Insights from the Texts of Consumers' Consumption Stories', *Journal of Marketing Research*, 34(4), 438-456
7. Thompson, C., Locander, W. and Pollio, H. (1989) 'Putting Consumer Experience Back into Consumer Research: The Philosophy and Method of Existential-phenomenology', *Journal of Consumer Research*, 16 (2), 133-147.

8. Venkatesh A. (1992) 'Postmodernism, Consumer Culture and the Society of the Spectacle', *Advances in Consumer Research*, 19, 199-202.
9. Schembri, S. and Sandberg, J. (2002) 'Service Quality and the Consumer's Experience: Towards an Interpretive Approach', *Marketing Theory*, 2(2): 189–205.
10. Lengnick-Hall, C., Claycomb, C. and Inks, L. (2000) 'From Recipient to Contributor: Examining Customer Roles and Experienced Outcomes', *European Journal of Marketing*, 343(3/4): 359–84.
11. Hamel, G. (1998) 'Strategy Innovation and the Quest for Value', *Sloan Management Review*, 39(2): 7–15.
12. Bettencourt, L. (1997) 'Customer Voluntary Performance: Customers as Partners in Service Delivery', *Journal of Retailing*, 73(3): 383–406.
13. Farrell, A., Souchon, A. and Durden, R. (2001), 'Service Encounter Conceptualisation: Employees' Service Behaviors and Customers' Service Quality Perceptions', *Journal of Marketing Management*, 17(5–6): 577–93.
14. Long-Tolbert, Till and Swaminathan (2006) Product Attribute Evaluations: Understanding the Role of Consumer Experience and Halo Effects, *Advances in Consumer Research*, 33, 678-679.
15. 'Vision Statements' from various company websites accessed 28th July, 2009.

8 How to Understand the Experiential Consumer

First and foremost it is necessary to appreciate the fact that understanding the experiential consumer at a rudimentary level requires no specialized skills. I have often found incredible amount of knowledge about the experiential consumer by just talking across a table with the marketing manager. So very often I have only had to sit and listen to CEOs and marketing managers and just provide pointers saying 'Hey! what you just mentioned is a potential experiential route!' It is but natural that those involved with their businesses should already possess several wonderful insights about what their consumers' experiences are with their offerings and how they can be enhanced. It is easy to pen down several experiential opportunities without added research and based on an organization's existing knowledge of the consumer. Unfortunately, few marketing managers are currently able to appreciate the experiential implications of what they already know, possibly because they are not thinking about EM at all. Once EM principles and its potential is understood, most managers will simply need to explicate their implicit knowledge of the consumer.

I also do not believe that a huge sample size is necessary before conclusions can be drawn about the experiential consumer. CEOs can walk in as mystery shoppers into kiranas, competing stores and their own service outlets and simply talk to consumers present there. If your antennae are sharp, if you have basics of marketing and consumer behaviour in place, if you can avoid being judgemental and can 'really listen' and 'observe', then you can be your own experiential researcher.

However, at times, it is useful to conduct dedicated experiential research to understand facets of the consumption process that are hidden from you (especially as related to pre-purchase, post-usage and disposal stages). Some commonly applicable techniques are briefly discussed below though each marketer needs to decide for oneself which method is likely to be most insightful depending on current business needs.

8.1 Personal Consumption Interviews

Personal Consumption Interviews are the most effective means to understand an individual consumer's interaction with the offering as it currently stands. One good route is to mentally walk with the consumer through the entire 'chronological route' of a specific purchase, to usage and disposal till next repurchase of the offering. The effort is to understand all three aspects:

(a) the consumption process and detailed steps in the process,

(b) the cognitive modes at each stage, and

(c) the emotional nodes at each stage.

Interviews that ask questions about consumption process are not a good route to explore identity and value related aspects. However, these consumption interviews can be used to generate a large amount of situational detail – the setting, the environment, moods, and other experiential aspects that are often useful for making experiential value additions and for planning experiential deliveries. The consumption interviews are also a fairly good way to explore the role of all five senses and understand the extent to which each sense was engaged, and if there is potential for increased engagement. Research has indicated that a sample size of as small as 35-40 is sufficiently rich to help a marketer with fantastic insights.

However, if the objective is to 'profile' one's consumers to identify 'experiential segments' then the sample size needs to be rather large. Research agencies specialized in qualitative techniques of interview can be asked to execute this though such agencies will need some input to help them understand your offerings experiential seek, related values and consumer identities.

8.2 Videos

Often I have noticed shoppers in stores walk in without picking up a trolley. They obviously have just a few items in mind and wish to move faster through the store (a cart will slow them down). After covering three or four aisles, they suddenly are turning their heads looking for a cart because they have picked up too many items by now. But they can never find that trolley for no store has consideration for such buyers.

I have also noticed several people abandon their shopping because a mobile call 'disrupted' their purchase process. As per my observational research estimates obtained from across 10 stores in two cities (Ahmedabad and Mumbai), this loss from 'shopping abandonment due to mobile-call disruptions' is almost as high as what stores lose every day through normal pilferage. A gentle intervention by a salesperson would have got most of these abandoners reinvolved in their purchases. But such efforts, these behaviours first need to be noticed and experientially interpreted.

Videos of consumption in action provide finer details of steps in the consumption process. Minor details cannot be covered in interviews.

8.3 Personal Script Interviews

In some cases, asking a direct question regarding the meaning of consumer's values tends to work. Though usually, the interviewee is uncomfortable speaking about such a core aspect of own one's self to a perfect stranger. The script interview is an alternative route to understand the 'meaning of experiences' for a consumer. The life-script associates itself well with the identity and values of the consumer. In this process, interviewee is asked to name a character or person – from mythology, comic books, panchatantra tales, reel or real life characters, who the person considers as rather similar to own self. The character description is sought in an exploratory manner and the interviewee is encouraged to describe values of the character and similarities with one's own self. Once similarity has been established, various aspects of the personality, life story, critical beliefs and attitudes etc., of the character are easier to obtain (people love talking about their scripts!).

Script interviews need some skills because it is a human tendency to become judgemental when people are talking about what they admire and respect. It is often difficult for a researcher to keep his own 'view of how to live life' out of the interview. Another caveat is regarding over-estimating one's own capability to empathize and trying to 'fill in' the blanks based on assumptions about what the researcher thinks the interviewee means. The purpose of the experiential researcher should be to ask (not make attributions) and clarify (not become questioning) in a completely non-threatening environment. A sample size of 35-40 has by and large been considered sufficient for exploring key consumer values and identities for any specific offering/ brand.

8.4 Ethnography

All the above information needs to be interpreted using the cultural context of the consumer. Respondents have a way of expressing themselves using phrases and gestures which cannot be aseptically analysed from an objective-analytical perspective. It requires cultural interpretation. Ethnography helps a marketer to explore associations between brand and consumer personalities. It allows for a culturally-anchored interpretation of all consumer related data – including what one reads on internet blogs. Ethnography is the method used to interpret expressions and phrases gathered during interviews, the behaviour captured on videos and all discussions read on the internet, etc. including images, written and verbalized words, in a culturally anchored way. The researcher uses knowledge of cultural artifacts (symbols) associated at each step of the consumption process and also interprets the consumption situation 'ethnographically'.

Ethnography has become a key method of understanding a consumer within a given cultural context. Several research agencies seem to confuse 'ethnography' to mean data on detailed consumer behaviour. That is incorrect. Behavioural data procurement (however innovative) is not ethnography. Ethnography is the process of interpreting and sorting out the meanings and expressions of consumers to unravel consumption truths for a marketer. It involves subjectivity of the researcher who is interpreting the meanings and therefore requires strong cultural knowledge about the research regarding the consumer's world. Organizations operating in India that hire 'culturally' different researchers who have no knowledge about Indians, let alone the regional and local differences across India (just because the parent company of that organization is in the US or UK), for conducting ethnographic studies for their Indian consumers are well advised to question the 'truths' furnished to them. Ethnographic 'truths' are not verifiable. The only verifiability often is an expensive strategic failure.

Ethnography is also different from anthropology though sometimes the two are confused to mean the same. The latter examines a group of people to understand their culture and behaviour by 'being invisible' – the researcher would try to blend into the group and 'live' the consumers' experiences. On the other hand, ethnography is comparatively a more applied research technique which has witnessed explosive growth along with EM. Ethnography does not require a researcher to be invisible and is not as time consuming as an anthropological study. It however helps to have an anthropologist as an added help to interpret findings from an ethnographic study. Most large organizations in the US either employ agencies to conduct regular ethnographic studies or have in-house facilities. One can expect a similar trend in India fairly soon.

8.5 Means-end Chain Analysis

Though it is considered a separate interview approach by itself, the means-end chain analysis is actually a technique of putting together all the insights given above meaningfully. The (interview) analysis is performed in a laddering manner. First you ask the consumer for and pen down all behavioural aspects in the consumption process. Then each behaviour is linked with experiential cues (touch, smell, sight, hearing and taste). Each cue is associated with specific-consumer attitudes. The attitudes are then hooked up with beliefs which then are progressively linked upwards with values and identities of the consumer. The means-end chain analysis provides a route by which behavioural aspects of consumption can be connected through a systematic laddering process right up till the values and identities of the consumers. Figure 8.1 shows an illustration of the laddering process involved in a means-end chain analysis for one single consumer. This interview was anchored to a brand that the consumer feels most loyal towards.

The means-end chain analysis is one useful way of pictorially representing the entire chain of associations obtained from personal interviews – both consumption related and script related. A completed means-end chain analysis provides a snapshot of the key experiential route to most of your consumers' values/identity (and which values/identity are occuring most in harmony with your offering).

Figure: 8.1 An illustration of the laddering interview process

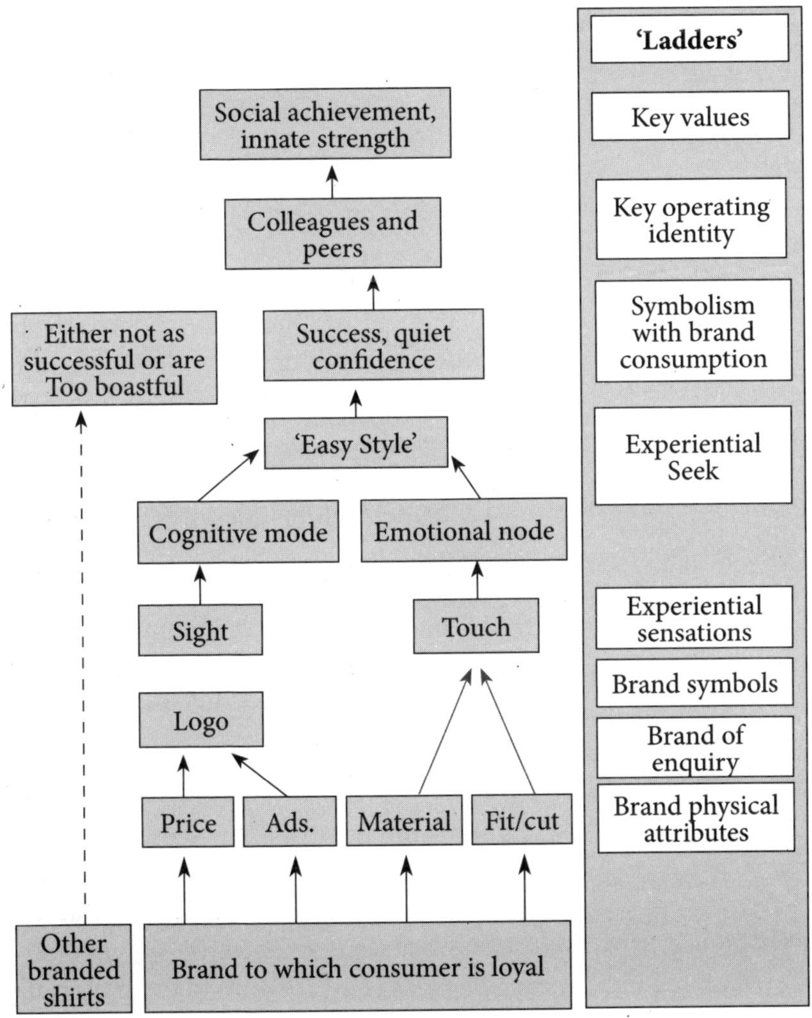

References

1. Malefyt, Timothy de Waal 'Understanding the Rise of Consumer Ethnography: Branding Technomethodologies in the New Economy. *American Anthropologist*, 111(2), 201-210

2. Kaul, Subhashini and Mehta, Nirmesh (2009), Note on Experiential Marketing, Working Paper IIMA, MARO0408 TEC